T0385102

AUSTIN MAHONE

Just How It Happened

My Official Story

SPHERE

Copyright © 2014 by A.M. Music, LLC
Cover photograph © Howard Huang
Cover design by Ian McAllister
Cover © 2014 Hachette Book Group, Inc.
Interior Design by Sasha Illingworth

The moral right of the author has been asserted.

A CIP catalogue record for this book is available from the British Library.

ISBN 978-0-7515-5620-9

Printed in the United States of America

Sphere
An imprint of
Little, Brown Book Group
100 Victoria Embankment
London EC4Y 0DY

An Hachette UK Company
www.hachette.co.uk
www.littlebrown.co.uk

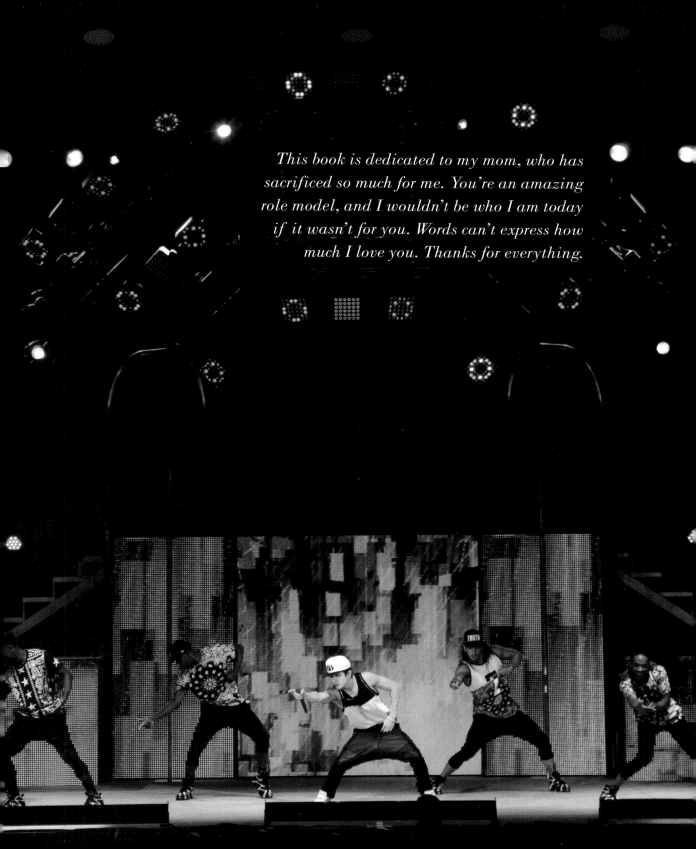

This book is dedicated to my mom, who has sacrificed so much for me. You're an amazing role model, and I wouldn't be who I am today if it wasn't for you. Words can't express how much I love you. Thanks for everything.

Contents

RIGHT FOOT IN   1

1. SECRET FAMILY RECIPE   13

2. THE CREW   33

3. SHOOT US DOWN   43

4. PLAYLIST LIVE   55

5. ALL IN   69

6. FINALLY   87

7. SAY SOMETHIN   101

8. FIRSTS   115

9. FAN FAVORITE   127

10. UPS AND DOWNS AND UPS   143

11. HEADLINER   165

12. HOMECOMING   177

SHOWTIME   197

AUSTIN MAHONE

Just How It Happened

My Official Story

Welcome to the backstage.

If you know one thing about me it's how much I love my fans. You are the ones who make it all possible. You allow me to go out there every day and live my dream, make my music, and perform around the world.

You're like my family.

You were there to wish me well when I got sick and had to postpone my first headlining tour, the MTV Artist to Watch Tour. You cheered me up while I was recovering. You've kept me company when I've been bored out of my mind during so many long hours alone in my room. Best of all, you've been there to celebrate with me during so many big firsts—my first show, first single release, first time on national TV, first time traveling out of the country, first time eating sushi, first award, etc.

So I think it's time for you to learn a little more about me and meet the rest of my family. Not just my mom. You know her already.

I mean the family that's always right there with me—and with you, really, since you're always right there with me, too—keeping me company on the road, in good times and bad.

See, my whole camp is one big family. I know people always say that. But sometimes I feel like, in a lot of other people's camps, they don't really pay attention to what's going on with each other. They'll do their individual parts to put on the show, and to make things look good while the cameras are on, but that's it. That's not us at all.

Our bond is close. Before the show, after the show, we're hanging out. We're going to the movies together. We're playing basketball backstage. We really do care about each other like family, and so, most important, these are the people who'll tell me if I look dumb, or need to work harder.

We have this tradition before every show. It started way back in the beginning, when it was just my mom and me. It's grown a lot since then, but the basic idea's the same: The last thing I do before every show, no matter where I am, and whether I'm playing for a few hundred Mahomies or for thousands, is to get everyone together backstage for a prayer circle.

Tonight's gathering is major because we're not playing just anywhere. We're in San Antonio, Texas, the place I was born and raised. I live in Florida now, but wherever I go, Texas will always be my home.

It's July 25, 2014. I'm playing at the Freeman Coliseum, where I used to come so many times as a kid to see the rodeo with my family, and then, when I was a little older, to watch from way up in the nosebleed section as some of my friends took part in cheer competitions. Not only is this a homecoming, but it's the first night of my first

2

national headlining tour—we're heading out for thirty dates in the next forty-five days, and I wouldn't want to kick it off anywhere else.

Looking around me, I could be backstage at any concert hall in the world. They all start to look the same after a while—industrial gray cement columns and floors, enormous empty spaces we've stuffed with all the equipment and people that go into putting on a huge live music show. The room we're in is made for hanging out, I guess—couches, carpet, some food—but nothing on the road really feels like home. That's why the people around me are so important. Along with my fans, they're my home, no matter how long it's been since I've seen my own bedroom in Miami, or how long it'll be until I'm back there again.

It's ten minutes or so before showtime. The opening acts just went out there and did their thing. I watched their sound checks earlier today. It wasn't that long ago that I was the one in the opening slot, warming up crowds for Taylor Swift or the big names on the Jingle Ball Tour last year, like Miley Cyrus. I know what it feels like to want to make the most of your time onstage. We're all here together to make some music and have a good time. The energy in the building is incredible already. I can't wait to get out there.

But first it's time to stop a minute and be grateful for everyone and everything it's taken to get here, and to focus on what we're about to do. Tonight it's an extra special ring of people because it contains nearly everybody who helped me to get where I am today.

We gather in close and put our arms around each other. My whole management team is here: Rocco Valdes, Michael Blumstein, David Abram, and Brian Spirio. They're all like father figures to me, or at least big brothers,

3

depending on the day. Along with my mom, these guys are always looking out for me.

Mike's always the one who leads our prayer circle. Mike's got that dad humor that's so bad, it's good, you know what I mean? It's kind of corny. All our friends make fun of his jokes and how bad they are. Like I said, we have a good time, which is important. We spend a lot of time together.

Nothing on the road really feels like home. That's why the people around me are so important. Along with my fans, they're my home.

"Right foot in," Mike says.

I stick out my right foot, in a red-and-black Jordan, which is what I usually like to wear when I'm performing because it's such a big, thick shoe and that makes it the best for doing things like toe spins (one of my favorite moves). Around me, a couple dozen right feet find their place in the center of the circle, too.

"We're here," Mike continues. "We've made it. This is two and a half years in the making to get to this building. Here we are, and it's sold out. Congrats, Austin."

Everyone around me claps and cheers. It feels amazing to hear this—*we sold out my hometown show*—and to have everyone get so excited.

"Thank you," I say. "Thank you."

WE'RE ALL HERE TOGETHER TO MAKE SOME MUSIC AND HAVE A GOOD TIME.

Next, Dave jumps in. "My man," he says, looking at me. "That's right. Let's give him a little, right? Right?" he adds, clapping louder.

The applause builds—it's already lifting me up, and I haven't even gotten out onstage yet, where the cheering will really be next-level.

"It's the first show of thirty," Mike says, giving us the pep talk I know is coming. "Thirty shows. We'll count them down from here. Show one, everyone. We've got a long tour. We'll be on the road for almost two months. Behave. Be safe. Don't get hurt. But give it a hundred and fifty million percent out there."

Everyone laughs. See? Dad joke. But also true. That's the goal, always.

"Big percentage, man," Dave says. "That's a big percentage."

We laugh harder. Having the right team means it's all fun, even the moments in between the big moments—just like family, we're always here for each other.

"Michele?" Dave says, handing the speech off to my mom.

I can tell my mom's feeling kind of emotional as she looks around at this big family we've built, and I know why. She's given so much to me already. She quit her job in 2011 to help me post videos on YouTube, not even because I had an actual music career or anything like that, just videos on YouTube. It was nuts. And not that long ago. Back then, it was just me and her, traveling together, making decisions together, doing it all together. But we always believed, just like you always believed.

You always know if you find me, my mom's right there with me, or not too far away. And here we are, together, surrounded by everyone who's come on board to help us.

"Well, I just want to say it's really very surreal for me, and I'm sure for Austin," she says. "This is his hometown, born and raised in San Antonio. We've been looking forward to this for a long time, so I'm excited. Everyone just have a great time tonight."

Mike looks to the next person in line to speak: my grandfather, who's been there for my mom and me since the very beginning, and who everyone in my extended family calls by the same name I do, like we really are one big family.

"Granddad, you got anything?" Mike asks.

"Welcome home," Granddad says, looking at me. "Welcome home."

"There it is," Mike says.

Now it's my turn. I look around the circle. There's my original crew—Robert, AC, and Zach—who have been my best friends since junior high. They don't say much in situations like this, but you'll hear more from them later on. They travel with me everywhere I go, and they're a huge part of everything I do.

My dancers, who've worked so hard leading up to this tour, and who spend so much time with me—the reason it looks like we're boys onstage is because we are; my musical director and right-hand man, Abe Poythress;

my choreographer, Nick DeMoura; his assistant, Aubree; my head of wardrobe, Natasha Herron; my mom's sister, my aunt Lisa; and my mom's long-time friend Ann Attridge, who now works as her assistant and keeps us all together on the road; my head of venue security, Seth; and then my head of security, Joe. He doesn't say much. He's real serious. But when you get to know him, he's probably the funniest guy you ever met, actually. If it weren't for Joe, the road would be really boring.

I told you it takes a lot of people to put on a show, didn't I? And that's not even including the production crew, venue personnel, and the dozens of people who have fed us and helped us to get this thing set up since we rolled into San Antonio five days ago to rehearse and prepare for the adventure ahead. All I can think as I get ready to speak is *This is awesome.*

"All right, let's go out there, guys, and have fun with it," I say. "I can't believe we really sold this place out. Let's show everyone out there why we're stars. And I know there's some people out there that aren't Mahomies, too. So let's make them Mahomies."

Finally, it's time for Josh, who was one of my first dancers. He has since become kind of like my dance captain and big brother. He came in and auditioned, like everyone else, but we just kind of clicked more than the rest, and we get along really great. He teaches me dance moves. But he teaches me everything really: stage presence, how I walk onstage, how I talk onstage—all that stuff, too. It's more like a brotherhood now. He's the only performer who has been with me from the beginning—well, at least the part of the beginning where I could afford to start hiring people, which was definitely not the *beginning* beginning. And Josh is the one we turn to now for the actual prayer.

"All right, bow your heads," Josh says. "Dear Lord, I want to start off by saying thank you for getting us to this point, and to this moment in all of our lives, and Austin's. Let him be the star that he is. Let everyone know that he is amazing, and he is going to shine no matter what happens in his lifetime." Before he wraps up, Josh gives a shout-out to everyone in the circle and everyone on the team not in the circle. "We have the best team. We all work together. And it's going to be great. Let's have fun."

Around the circle, people say, "Amen," and we all throw our hands into the center, one on top of another, like a team huddle. That's right, you get in there, too. You're with us now.

"You ready?" Mike asks, surveying all of us.

We all nod. *We are ready.*

"Turn up!" Mike shouts, drill sergeant–style.

"Right now!" we shout back, getting ourselves worked up for the stage.

"Turn up!"

"Right now!"

"Turn up!"

"Right now!"

"Awww…Booommm…Ssshhh."

We all pull our hands out at the same time to make a shushing gesture, and then we clap as loud as we can. It's showtime.

Music and family are probably the two biggest constants in my life. For me, when I was growing up at least, family meant my mom, granddad, and mema, which is the word we use for grandma down south, like you might call your grandmother Granny or Grams. I only knew my dad through the stories I've heard from my mom and his family about him being a really hard worker and a cowboy in the rodeo. He took his life when I was sixteen months old, so I don't remember him. Because it happened when I was so young, I don't miss him or feel sad about it in the ways you might think. It's something that happened to us, and my mom, being as strong as she is, never let me feel like there was a void.

My family is amazing, and we've always had the best time together. When I was really little, my mom and I lived with my granddad and mema. And then, when I got older and we moved out into our own house, we still had all these family traditions I loved. Like every Thanksgiving, Mom and I would stay over, and

1. SECRET FAMILY RECIPE

my mema would wake up way before us in the morning and bake this special golden braid bread from a secret family recipe. And I mean she made it from scratch, by hand, without a bread machine or anything, which is probably why it always tasted so good. The rest of us woke up early, too, but she was always way ahead of the game, so the first thing I noticed as I stretched out in my bed on Thanksgiving morning was this amazing smell—baking bread. It's the best smell ever.

We'd all meet up in the living room, still in our pajamas, and pile onto the couch together to watch the Macy's Thanksgiving Day Parade on TV. Mema timed it perfectly so the bread was ready just when we were gathering in the living room. She cut off these big chunks of the braid for us, and we'd eat it fresh out of the oven with lots of butter and jam. So good.

Granddad always sat in his special chair and read the newspaper. And Mom sat next to me on the couch, drinking her coffee. Mema was in and out of the kitchen the whole time, and more good smells came as the day wore on—roasting ham and turkey and the sugary sweetness of fresh-baked pies (apple pie with cinnamon was my favorite).

We'd watch the parade until every last bit of it had gone by, the marching bands and the singers performing on floats as they slowly glided through the big city, which was so far away from us in San Antonio. You could see thousands of people on TV, lining the streets, all bundled up in their winter coats and hats, even though I was wearing shorts back in Texas. I wanted to go there one day, to New York City. I wanted to *be* one of those people watching the balloons and floats.

My granddad and I usually spent Thanksgiving afternoon throwing a football around in the yard, or just hanging out, talking. And then, around four or five, we would all sit down together to eat. As I got older I discovered another favorite Thanksgiving food: green bean casserole.

I'll tell you a funny story. Last year, the editors at *M* magazine were doing a special holiday feature on the dishes artists love best. I was going on and on to the reporter about my mema's green bean casserole. And so the magazine got in touch with my mom and asked her if they could include our delicious family recipe so all of you could enjoy it at home with your families. My mom started laughing and then broke the news to them, and to me, that our amazing secret family recipe was actually the Campbell's recipe from a can of cream of mushroom soup. Hahahaha. Still tasted good to me.

I used to go to my grandparents' house all the time, not just on Thanksgiving, and Granddad taught me so many things. He was basically like my dad. He was the one who took me out into the yard and showed me how to play football and baseball. He also taught me the stuff that I can see now is really important in life, like how to be respectful of people.

Granddad is one of those people who's friendly and outgoing and can make everyone he meets feel special and good. He showed me how, when I'm in a new place or a new social situation, I should go up to all the

16

people who are there and shake hands and say hello. He even had me do it with other little kids.

There was this playground near their house. And of course I always wanted to go on the swings and the slide. If we were driving by, and he saw other children my age playing on the equipment, he'd pull the car over.

"Let's go meet them," he'd say, pointing.

And we would. I made some of my earliest friends that way.

My mom definitely taught me good things, too, like manners, but she's a little more shy. Because my granddad was so outgoing and easy to be around, everyone always had a positive reaction to meeting him, and that taught me how important it is to make an effort to be polite to people and just be friendly. So if you've ever met me, and we had a good conversation, you have my granddad to thank for that.

Growing up, I was always singing in the car and around the house. I actually love singing more than almost anything else. It feels so great, and it always has, even when I had no idea what I was doing or even if I was any good or not. It just made me happy. In fact, we have a family picture that I know my mom would say is really cute. I have no clue if it is. I mean I don't look at my old baby pictures and say, "Aw, look at that cute kid." But I do think it's a cool picture because it shows where it all started. I'm on this makeshift stage (which was actually a step stool) in my granddad

and mema's living room, singing into a mic. I can't remember which song—it was a long time ago. But it goes to show how much I've always loved singing and performing—I was doing it before I even remember doing it.

I guess my mom could tell music was really important to me, because she and everyone else in my family always encouraged me to do it. I started taking piano lessons when I was six. But my teacher was really strict. I remember thinking, *This is not fun. I don't want to do this.* So I stopped.

Even when I wasn't playing anything specific, my mom and I sang in the car together all the time. She'd be in the front seat, driving, and I'd be in the back in my car seat, and we'd both be belting it out. She was in choir when she was in middle school, so I probably even learned a few things from her right in the beginning.

When my mom and I were singing in the car together, we were usually singing country. That's what was on the radio, and that's what my mom would put on when we were home, so that's what I listened to growing up: George Strait, Alan Jackson, Rascal Flatts, Garth Brooks, Kenny Chesney, Tim McGraw. My favorite song to sing back then was by Alan Jackson—"Where I Come From"—probably because of its line about corn bread and chicken, which I loved to eat. I was five at the time, but I still love it. He had that extra twang in his voice, and we always had fun copying that, making our voices have as much twang as we could, singing all the lyrics, and laughing at how "country" we could sound.

Now you might already know this, but there is one place in particular where I've always loved to sing more than any other: in the shower. There's just something about the acoustics in the bathroom that sound so good. Even now, when I warm up with my vocal coach, I go into the bathroom by myself to sing by the row of sinks, and there's just something about the way my voice echoes off the tiles that's amazing. Back then, I wasn't warming up for anything, but I'd sing in any and every shower, without even thinking about it.

One time when I was seven, my mom and I were visiting her friend in Orlando, and I was singing in the shower in Spanish, a language I don't even speak—it just sounds so great, even if you don't know what the words mean. My mom heard me, and she thought it was so funny. She took a video of just my head peeking out of the shower curtain, wailing away in

iend's shower like I was a Tejano star. That's one video you'll nev
YouTube.

---

efore I played any instruments, my mom took me to hang out a
sic store in San Antonio because I loved it so much. That's wher
ienced love at first sight. I was only seven years old, but I knew it
felt it.

ally from the moment I walked in, it was like everything else fell
there was no one but us in the room: just me and this beautiful,
...drum kit. As soon as I saw it I had to have it. I knew it was a
especially because my grandparents had given me my first guitar
tmas the year before—a sparkly green Ibanez electric guitar. I

EVEN BEFORE I PLAYED ANY INSTRUMENTS, MY MOM TOOK ME TO HANG OUT AT THE MUSIC STORE IN SAN ANTONIO BECAUSE I LOVED IT SO MUCH.

never played it. I thought it was a really cool gift. I just didn't pick it up that much. But this drum kit, now this was perfect, shiny and red, with all these cymbals, a snare—and I couldn't stop thinking about it. I'd had a toy drum kit when I was really little, and I'd always loved to smash away on it. But this was the real deal.

On Christmas morning that year, I could hardly wait to get out to the Christmas tree and see if my wish had come true. I practically ran down the hallway. And there it was: my drum kit. I was so happy. That was the first instrument I actually enjoyed playing, and I played it all the time.

My first crystal clear memory of playing music is banging on that drum kit, right there on Christmas morning. I'd barely gotten it unwrapped, and

it was practically underneath the Christmas tree, with all these gift boxes and big piles of crumpled-up wrapping paper everywhere. But I couldn't wait, and I was already up on the drum stool, with the sticks in my hands. It just felt right, like that was my own little world, and it was exactly where I belonged. My mom, granddad, and mema were my first audience, and they all sat there, smiling at me, always so supportive, even though I'm sure it was nothing but noise. I guess they were just glad to see me enjoying myself, and they didn't care how bad it sounded.

I certainly didn't know how to play back then. I just liked to fool around and see what I could do. I think the first beat I ever learned was the "We Will Rock You" beat. You know the one: Doom doom dat. Doom doom dat. I still remember it.

After Christmas, I set my drums up in the living room, and I played all the time. I'm sure *that* wasn't annoying. (Sorry, Mom!)

My mom got me drum lessons for a year from this cool bald guy who lived a few subdivisions over from us. He kept it simple because I was a kid, and I was just learning, but little by little, he taught me a lot.

The first time I ever performed in front of anybody besides my family was my elementary school talent show when I was nine or ten. I played a long drum solo for everybody. My favorite drummer at that time was Tommy Lee from Mötley Crüe. I'd like to think I channeled some of his playing, but you know, what really matters is that I had fun. I know that sounds cheesy, but it's true! Drums are fun, and I still love to play them.

Even though I played drums most of the time, my grandparents always encouraged me to play guitar. After all, they'd bought me that guitar I'd asked for, and they'd never seen me play it (now that I think about it, they

I FEEL LIKE ALL MUSIC IS THE SAME, WHEN YOU GET DOWN TO BASICS. IT'S ABOUT COMMUNICATING EMOTION. AND THAT'S WHAT I LOVE ABOUT IT SO MUCH. I WOULDN'T WANT TO SPEND MY LIFE ANY OTHER WAY.

were probably just trying to get me to stop playing the drums, the loudest instrument of all time). I used to go to their lake house in the summer, and they happened to have a neighbor who was a guitar player, and so they asked him if he could teach me a few things. He never gave me official lessons or anything, but he taught me the basics—you know, just enough to be able to mess around a little bit. At that point, though, drums were still my first love.

When I was fourteen, my mom and I decided we were going to take guitar lessons together. My mom had always wanted to learn how to play guitar, and she liked to encourage my love of music, so she eventually

24

convinced me that it would be a fun mom-and-son thing to do. I know, maybe that's not the coolest way to learn guitar, but what can I say? My mom's the best, and I like to make her happy. So that year, my mom bought me another guitar—my first acoustic guitar. I played it a lot, and I've never stopped.

The whole idea of taking lessons with my mom didn't last long, though. We found this guitar teacher named Manny and started out by sharing an hour lesson together every week, but I learned so much so fast that we split up after a month and each had our own half-hour lesson. A month later, my mom gave me the whole hour. She hasn't taken guitar lessons since, but I was immediately hooked.

The first song I ever learned to play on guitar was "More Than Words" by Extreme. My mom never had to force me to practice. I played all the time. Not long after that, when I was fifteen, I picked up piano again, but for real this time. And now I play a little ukulele, too, because I got one as a thank-you gift when I was on this show called *Teen Hoot*. You never know when you're going to need to bust out a little ukulele.

The second song I learned on guitar was by, yes, one of San Antonio's main claims to fame: George Strait. I'm from Texas, and there's nothing but country music out there, so I got into it. Every now and then, growing up, I'd hear some Akon or Ne-Yo, but mainly, it was country.

My first concert that I ever went to was a Kenny Chesney concert when I was ten, and you might not believe this, but I didn't go to any other concert until I started performing at them five years later. That's probably because I got into other music soon after that, and, like I said, there was mainly country music where I lived, so the artists I liked didn't come through on tour that much.

One day when I was twelve or thirteen, I was hanging out with some friends, and I heard T-Pain for the first time. Immediately, I was like, *Oh, man, what's this? This is so different from what I'm used to listening to, and I love it.* By this time, I wanted something new, so I started listening to more R&B and hip-hop. From there, I started listening to Lil Wayne, Chris Brown, Drake, and all those guys.

At the time, I thought country and R&B were totally different worlds, but now that I actually spend most of my life singing and writing and thinking about music, I can see they're kind of similar. Before you say I'm crazy, think about this: In country music, the singers are really soulful, and you can just hear all the emotion in their voices. They mean everything they say. And R&B is the same way. It's like every note, every word, is telling you exactly how the singers feel about what they're singing about. It's just that in country music, all that feeling is usually about a truck, and in R&B, it's more often about a girl. And for me, girls are a lot more fun to sing about than a truck.

All joking aside, I feel like all music is the same, when you get down to basics. It's about communicating emotion. And that's what I love about it so much. I wouldn't want to spend my life any other way. These days, I'm into all types of music: rock, R&B, pop, country, hip-hop, jazz, classical, Tejano... anything, really.

I guess I was always looking beyond what was right in front of me. I wanted to listen to and play music that wasn't the normal Texas thing. More than that, I wanted to see the world beyond my hometown. My family lives in all different places. My dad's family is in Houston, so we used to go there to see them at Christmas and during the summer. (We still go a couple times

I guess I was always looking beyond what was right in front of me.

a year to visit my nana and aunt Robin. That's when I get to hang out with my cousins Logan and Rylie.) And we also have relatives in Pennsylvania and Florida, so we'd visit them sometimes when I was growing up, too. No matter where we were going or how long we were staying, I always loved flying and going to new places.

There was one place I really wanted to go, more than any other: New York City. Maybe it was from watching the Macy's Thanksgiving Day Parade on TV for all those years, or because I knew so much amazing music and culture and food came out of there, but that was always it for me, and I just had to see it for myself someday. Finally, in the summer of 2010, my granddad took me on a trip to NYC, just me and him.

We had a great time. We walked around, checking out everything, got some classic New York City hot dogs from a street vendor, and saw the Statue of Liberty. Best of all, we spent time with my mom's first cousin Mac Demy. He's a real musician with a small studio in his

IT WAS LIKE THIS WHOLE NEW WORLD OPENED UP FOR ME, AND I WANTED TO FIND A WAY TO JOIN IT.

apartment and an album available on iTunes. I was immediately into learning everything about his musical career. It was like this whole new world opened up for me, and I wanted to find a way to join it. He even said I should write a few songs and come back and record them the next summer.

The whole time I was there, I had so much energy. It was like the best place in the world, and I wanted more and more.

"I love New York," I told Granddad. "I want to come back again."

Granddad smiled at me before he said anything. It was a smile he gave when he was worried about disappointing me.

"It's going to be hard," he said. "It's expensive. You might not come back for a long, long time."

I nodded and took that in. I knew my mom had always worked hard for everything we had, and that Granddad and Mema helped us out, too. And I knew soon I'd be working at something. But I was determined I'd get back there before long.

And, man, when I finally did, it was even better than I could have ever

dreamed. But that was the amazing thing about my family: Even when something seemed kind of far-off, and maybe impossible, they always let me know it might be hard to get there, it might take work, but I should always dare to dream. And so now that it's paying off, I feel like all of this is for them as much as it is for me. It makes everything that's happened even better.

W hen I was growing up, I never thought much about living in San Antonio, or whether or not I liked it there. It was just where I lived, and I liked where I lived. It was where my family, my friends, and the music store I loved were, and that was all I needed.

And then my mom got remarried, and the summer before I started sixth grade, we moved to this little town called La Vernia, which is about forty-five minutes outside of San Antonio. I'd liked my school in San Antonio and had a lot of friends there, so I was nervous about making this big change. But my mom reminded me that I would have ended up going to a different school from most of my friends for junior high anyhow, and she told me that she'd drive me back to San Antonio to keep up my drum lessons, and to see my friends anytime I wanted. Plus, she was really into the idea of me having a country childhood and kept telling me how great it was going to be. I did like the house we were building in La Vernia, which was big enough to

2. THE CREW

have a music room where we kept our piano and my drums, and which was on a cul-de-sac where I could ride my bike and skateboard. It also had a tree house and a trampoline, so by the time we moved, I was pretty excited.

Now, the funny thing about growing up in Texas is that people who aren't from there just assume we ride horses to school and do all this weird stuff, like we're living in a rodeo every day of our lives, when of course that's not true.

Or at least that's what I'd always thought. And then I moved to La Vernia, which is like a scene out of a country song. All you see on the road are trucks, and everyone wears Wranglers with a can of dip in their back pocket and cowboy boots and hats—not just on special occasions, but every single day.

Maybe it was because I was really getting into hip-hop and R&B, while everyone there was so into country music—it was a way of life there—or maybe I'm just different in general, but I never felt like I fit in from the first day I started school. And as time went on, that didn't change.

Luckily, that summer my mom had signed me up for Pop Warner football. We started practicing before the beginning of the school year, so I met all the kids on my team before I met anyone else. And that's where I met Robert Villanueva. Robert and I hit it off right away, which was great, because when I started sixth grade in September, I had at least one friend. And that made a big difference.

We lived in La Vernia for four and a half years. That first year I was there, our football team went to nationals in Florida, where we came in second. So Robert and I had that whole experience together, and it created a kind of brotherly bond. I played linebacker. I would rather have

played wide receiver because I like to catch, but I still really liked to play, and it was great to be on such a good team. Going through all of that with Robert—playing that whole season, going to Florida with the team, and then *losing*—meant we had something in common for life.

But even though I was friends with Robert when school started, it was still a tough time. I don't know about you, but for me, sixth grade was rough. None of the kids were into the same music or clothes as me. And that was fine with me, but it mattered to them.

It got to the point where I looked forward to my visits to Granddad and Mema's, not only because I loved hanging out with them but also because I could relax there and not worry about some kid looking at me funny or calling

me names, just because I liked sneakers instead of cowboy boots. I pretended that getting teased didn't bug me, but of course it did back then.

Right before seventh grade, I went to visit Granddad and Mema. By then, they had moved to Dallas for a couple years for Grandad's work. The hottest shoes that year were Nike Shox. I had wanted them for the longest time. And there they were at the shoe store in the mall in Dallas, right there in the display window, and in the colors I wanted, too: blue and silver. La Vernia didn't have shoe stores like this, so I'd never seen them in person. They looked so cool. Granddad and Mema had already walked on to the next store, but I stayed behind, practically drooling. I walked into the store to get a better look and picked them up. Granddad followed me over to the display and had a look for himself.

"I need these shoes," I said, still holding one, unable to put it down.

He looked at the sticker on the bottom. "Those are really expensive," he said.

"Please," I said.

We stood there looking at each other and at the shoe for a long time, and I thought maybe he was going to go for it because he hadn't said no yet. But then, finally, he shook his head. My heart sank, and I put the shoe back on the display. I didn't ask for a lot of things, so I'd hoped Granddad would see how much I needed these shoes.

I KNEW THERE WAS A WHOLE WORLD OUT THERE, WITH ALL DIFFERENT KINDS OF MUSIC AND PEOPLE, AND I KNEW I WAS GOING TO GET OUT OF THIS SMALL TOWN SOMEDAY AND JOIN IT.

"Let me think about it," he said.

We walked around the mall some more, and I tried to forget about the shoes, but I couldn't.

As we were getting ready to leave, Mema turned to Granddad and said, "This is a special trip for Austin, and those shoes seem really important to him."

I kept quiet but was hopeful as Mema paused to look at me.

Then she said, "We need to go back and get those shoes."

Yes, Mema!

As soon as I put those shoes on, they felt perfect and looked so cool. Right then and there, my shoe obsession began. My Shox were one of the most important items of clothing I've ever owned, but for a different reason that at the time I just didn't know.

On the first day of school, I was so excited to wear my new Nike Shox. Not that I expected anyone else to appreciate them.

But when I was playing football that day, I saw this kid Alex Constancio. I'd seen him around before. It was a small school. But I'd never really talked to him. And he was wearing Nike Shox, too, only his were red and black.

"I like your shoes," I said.

We both looked down at our two pairs of Nike Shox, facing each other, and then looked up.

"I like yours, too," Alex said.

And that's how I met one of my best friends for life. Don't ever let anyone tell you that shoes aren't important, because they are.

Alex and I were different, and everyone knew it. We didn't mind being different. But for some reason, in school, it seems like kids have this thing where they want everyone to be cool in the same way, and if you're not, they can't deal with it and give you a hard time.

Mostly, I just tried to stay out of it. It was like Alex and I were so completely different that they didn't know what to do with us. Which was fine by me. I just wanted to be left alone to listen to the music I liked and hang out with Alex and Robert, and Robert's friend Zach Dorsey, who also became a friend. It turned out that Alex and Zach had known each other since kindergarten, and they used to be close. But then they'd drifted apart in that way we do sometimes. And by the time we were in junior high, Robert and Zach were really close, and I was spending most of my time with Alex, or AC, as I started calling him, which is how you might know him, too. But then, because Robert and I had been such good friends in middle school, the four of us ended up hanging out together all the time.

Once that happened, and there were four of us instead of just two, it was like we were kind of a united front, and it didn't bother any of us so much that we were different. We were having too much fun to worry about the other kids. We spent a lot of time playing video games, or outside playing basketball, or riding our bikes and skateboarding, and I had this little go-kart we used to drive around my neighborhood. Plus, we just laughed all the time. Which of course is the best.

I didn't take any of the social stuff at school that seriously. My main way of dealing with it was this: I was really quiet in school. I sat in the back and watched everyone and didn't say much. But for some reason, the kind of kids who care about being popular in high school are never content to let you do your own thing.

As I got older, some kids still gave me a hard time about the way I dressed and the fact that I wasn't obsessed with the rodeo and country music like everyone else was.

The one good thing I can say about this time is that it made me get clear on something: Either they were right, or I was right. And I knew they weren't right. I knew there was a whole world out there, with all different kinds of music and people, and I knew I was going to get out of this small town someday and join it. And when I did, I was never going to look down on anyone. I was going to let everyone be who they wanted to be and not worry about it. I'd be too busy enjoying my life.

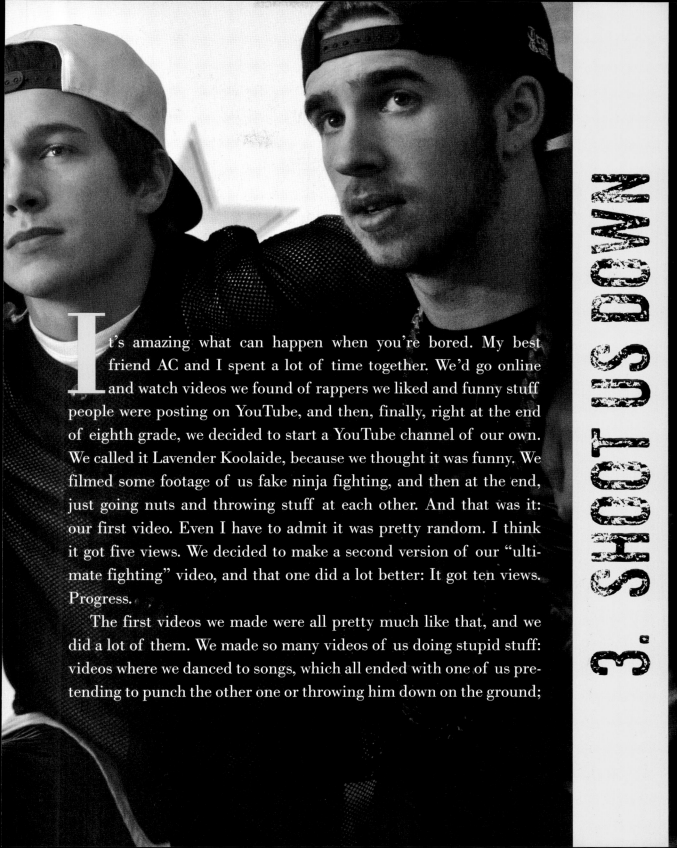

It's amazing what can happen when you're bored. My best friend AC and I spent a lot of time together. We'd go online and watch videos we found of rappers we liked and funny stuff people were posting on YouTube, and then, finally, right at the end of eighth grade, we decided to start a YouTube channel of our own. We called it Lavender Koolaide, because we thought it was funny. We filmed some footage of us fake ninja fighting, and then at the end, just going nuts and throwing stuff at each other. And that was it: our first video. Even I have to admit it was pretty random. I think it got five views. We decided to make a second version of our "ultimate fighting" video, and that one did a lot better: It got ten views. Progress.

The first videos we made were all pretty much like that, and we did a lot of them. We made so many videos of us doing stupid stuff: videos where we danced to songs, which all ended with one of us pretending to punch the other one or throwing him down on the ground;

videos of AC riding dirt bikes; videos of AC solving a Rubik's Cube (in one minute and five seconds—he's good). It's not like I'm embarrassed by anything stupid I've done in front of a camera, but let's just say I don't think it's the worst thing in the world that a lot of those first videos have been lost. In fact, we took some of them down ourselves because they were just so bad. No one was really watching anyhow back then, but it was fun.

That summer was my trip to NYC, and after I got back, I kept thinking about the time I'd spent hanging out with Mac while we were there. And how cool it would be to write songs and record them with him someday. But someday was a far-off thing, and I had this feeling of wanting to do something now.

That July, AC and I decided to get serious about what we were doing on YouTube. On July 10, 2010, we launched the channel that finally stuck, Shoot Us Down. We named it for this Lil Wayne song we liked, "Shoot Me Down." Only we called it "Shoot US Down," because there were two of us. Mostly we were still making random videos—they were almost like comedy skits of us play fighting, or just generally goofing around.

And then one day, I decided to sing for our next video. Even though I was interested in maybe getting into the music business like Mac, it wasn't

"Just the way you are" Bruno Mars Cover - 14 yr old Austin Mahone

like I thought I was a singer or anything. It just seemed like a cool thing to do.

We were sitting at AC's computer in his room, hanging out in front of his webcam, and I belted out Chris Brown's "With You" while AC lip-synched the words along with me. AC was in charge of the video, which is why he kept leaving the frame—he was trying to record us, too. That video did a little better than our skits, and that got our attention.

It's not like we expected anything to ever come of the videos, but we decided to see how many subscribers we could get, just for fun. We talked online with some other people who were into YouTube, and they told us that the way to get more subscribers and build our channel was to post new videos constantly. So that's what we did, and that's how we ended up doing more music videos. They were easy and fun and seemed to get a good response from people online. Plus, I really liked singing.

Then we got disciplined. We made a rule that we had to put up a new video every week. Also, now that we were actually trying to make our videos not be the worst and get people to see them, AC and I started thinking about how to get more views. One weekend when we were at my house, we had a brainstorm.

We printed out a thousand small flyers promoting our Shoot Us Down channel on YouTube, and we went into the kitchen to find my mom and ask her if she'd take us to the mall.

She was always good about driving me back to San Antonio, just like she'd promised when we first moved to La Vernia and I was nervous I'd miss my drum lessons and my friends. So of course she said yes. AC and I piled into the backseat of her car with this big stack of flyers. She drove us to North Star Mall in San Antonio, where we knew

that kids liked to hang out. She dropped us off and said she'd pick us up in a few hours.

We found an empty table at the food court and left a bunch of flyers, which were nothing fancy, just something to get our name out there: basic black and white with the words SHOOT US DOWN in big, bold letters across the top, and then a photo of us, and the link to our YouTube channel. We left them in stores. We even left them on the ground—anywhere we thought people might pick them up. The whole time, we were laughing and joking around with each other about the flyers, because we had no idea if they were going to cause anything to happen or if we were just wasting our time. But at least we were *trying* to make something happen.

On Monday after school, AC and I were in his room, as usual, when we went to our YouTube channel like we did every day. Only this time,

46

the page looked a little different. There were actually a bunch of comments now:

"I saw your flyer at the mall. I like your videos."

"Found your flyer. Cool videos."

We looked at each other and started laughing.

"Sweet, it worked," I said.

After that, we went to the mall every weekend we could get my mom to drive us. We'd always wanted to hang out there because there was nothing to do in La Vernia, but now it felt different. Like we were really doing something.

Then we noticed a change at the mall.

We were there one Saturday afternoon when a group of girls started following a little ways behind us, and they were clearly talking about us. We didn't recognize them from school, so we figured maybe they had us confused with some other guys they knew. We slowed down until they finally came up to where we were. One of the girls stepped in front of the others, and the rest of them laughed, like they were nervous.

"You're those two guys on YouTube who do the hilarious videos," she said.

At first I thought she was saying my singing was hilarious, as in bad, but then I figured she was giving us a compliment, so she must mean that she'd seen and liked the videos of us goofing around and having fun.

AC and I looked at each other. We had just met someone who liked what we were doing!

"Thanks for watching," I said, trying to be cool.

And then it hit us: We might have some fans. And they didn't just think we were funny, either. I could tell from the comments posted on our music videos that they really liked my singing. Not long after that, I was thinking about how some musicians had nicknames for their fans, like how the really big Justin Bieber fans were called Beliebers and Katy Perry fans were called KatyCats. And then it came to me. If I ever had a lot of fans, they would be Mahomies—you know, like my name, Mahone, and my friends, "my homies." I didn't think I'd ever have real fans, but hey, at least there were those girls at the mall. Maybe they could be Mahomies. AC and I joked a lot about having fans. Because who actually thinks something like that is going to happen to them?

Late that October, we did our first "real" music video, which was a version of "Waiting on the World to Change" by John Mayer. Whenever I sang, I wanted to sound good, and I always tried my best. But we'd never worried about whether our videos were professional looking. But for this shoot, we went all out. I pre-recorded myself singing the vocals, and then we had our friend Cameron—one of the other guys we hung out with besides Robert and Zach—record black-and-white footage of us walking around La Vernia. For the bridge, I "played" guitar (wearing sunglasses, of course) while AC "played" keyboard. We also did some dancing in his bedroom. It was fun.

Soon almost half the videos we posted were of me singing, and the rest were the other, random ones of us messing around. The singing ones definitely continued to get a better reaction, but we still didn't take any of them that seriously, at least at first: I'd be singing, and AC would be in the background somewhere, because he was still always in the videos with me.

The first song I sang on YouTube by myself, just so I could focus on my

48

singing a little bit more, was "Beautiful Soul" by Jesse McCartney. As AC clicked on the camera and the music started, I got an idea: I'd recently met this cute girl, Selena, at the beach, and I figured I knew how to impress her.

"This one's for you, Selena," I said.

And then I sang that song like I was singing it right to her. I don't know if Selena ever saw it—it certainly didn't lead to getting a date with her like I'd hoped. But that became something I did in videos. I liked the feeling of singing directly to someone—and it was at least a good way to make an impression on girls, if nothing else. Sometimes the girl who got the shout-out would watch, even if no one else did.

I started doing a cappella versions of songs a lot. I was also taking guitar lessons that fall, so I started to play the guitar in my videos, and then, eventually, the piano. The more videos we posted, the more popular our videos and our channel became, and the more subscribers we had.

Soon we weren't just noticing a change when we were at the mall. A week after one of our new videos went up, it had twenty views. And the next week it had a hundred. And then a thousand. And then two thousand. That was pretty crazy. I never in a million years thought our videos could lead me to travel the world, singing for people. So when all this first started to take me to where I am now, I couldn't believe how quickly it went from me and AC messing around on YouTube to me and AC posting a video that got thousands of views.

Unfortunately, it wasn't just my new fans who discovered my singing on YouTube. The kids at school knew about it, too, and they weren't impressed. Not shocking but still, it was so stupid. It seemed like every day I went to school, someone had to say something about the whole thing. I didn't understand why they even cared—it wasn't like I ever asked them to watch the videos. Especially if they didn't like them.

It was hard not to let it get to me, but I did my best to just ignore them. School was school, and then I'd go home or over to AC's to make new videos or hang out online, and we'd look at the increasing number of comments we were starting to get, and even interact with some of our new fans, which was so cool.

Then in November 2010, the town of La Vernia held its first annual talent show. I'd been working hard on my music, and I decided to go for it. I told Mom I wanted to enter. As usual, she was totally supportive. So was my guitar teacher, Manny, who worked with me to get ready. I practiced and practiced. When it was time to audition, I was picked.

A few days before the talent show, I went to a pep rally at school that also included a talent show. I really wanted to sing in that talent show, too. I knew I could nail it. Then I thought about how some of the kids always teased me, and I wondered if they would make fun of me more. Maybe they would, but then I thought: *Who cares?*

It felt amazing to realize that. Still, I was really nervous as I waited my turn. Finally, a teacher announced me. I had never sung live in front of anyone before, but I strolled out to the middle of the gym floor, took the mic, and started to sing an a cappella version of "I'll Be" by Edwin McCain.

Once I was into the song, I got caught up, like I did in front of a video camera. A few girls cheered. A few sang along. There's this way it feels when the audience is into the music and the moment—as a performer, you can always tell—and that started to happen in that gym. When I finished, this huge cheer erupted from all the girls.

50

But then
I thought:
Who cares?

It felt
amazing
to realize
that.

PEOPLE ARE GOING TO GIVE THEIR OPINIONS ABOUT YOU, I THOUGHT. SOME PEOPLE ARE GOING TO MAKE FUN OF YOU, NO MATTER WHAT. SO YOU MIGHT AS WELL DO WHATEVER YOU WANT AND ENJOY IT.

Of course, not everyone liked my performance—and one kid made a point of telling me so—but I didn't care. I had fun, and guess what...*I won*.

That weekend was the town talent show. For that one, I played my acoustic guitar and sang. I had just sung in front of a crowd for the first time at school, and now I was about to have another first, because I'd never played *and* sung onstage at the same time. But I didn't really get nervous. I was just excited to get out there and do it. This audience was a lot smaller, and a lot nicer, so I knew I had nothing to worry about.

There were at least fifteen acts, and I was the last one, so it felt like I had to wait forever. When it was finally my turn, I went out there, sat down on a stool, started strumming my guitar, and just went for it. I sang "So Sick" by Ne-Yo. Not only did I win the talent show, but I also, finally, felt like a real singer. I wasn't just singing in AC's bedroom anymore. I had an audience, and they were clapping for me. It felt amazing, and I knew I wanted to experience it again.

Sure, I'd started this for fun, but now that I saw there were so many views coming in—thousands and thousands for each video—and I was getting so many comments and so much feedback, I was taking it more seriously. I wanted to take all of this as far as I could and see where it might end up going.

Once I realized our channel was getting pretty big, and people seemed to like my singing, I decided to make a separate channel of just myself, just singing covers, so I could focus completely on the music. I talked to AC to make sure he was cool with this and to let him know even though I was doing something a little bit different now, we were still in this together. AC was such a good friend to me. He could see how things were developing for me, and he was totally supportive. Everyone should be so lucky as to have a best friend like him. I knew I was lucky to have him and Robert and Zach, even back then.

There were some dark days in school. Some people still made fun of me for my videos. I tried to hold on to the positive feedback, but sometimes it was impossible not to let the negative stuff get to me. *Maybe they're right*, I thought, when I heard some dudes talking about me. *Maybe I am stupid for putting myself on YouTube.* But luckily, there was something inside of me that wouldn't let me believe that. *People are going to give their opinions about you*, I thought. *Some people are going to make fun of you, no matter what. So you might as well do whatever you want and enjoy it.*

So that's what I did.

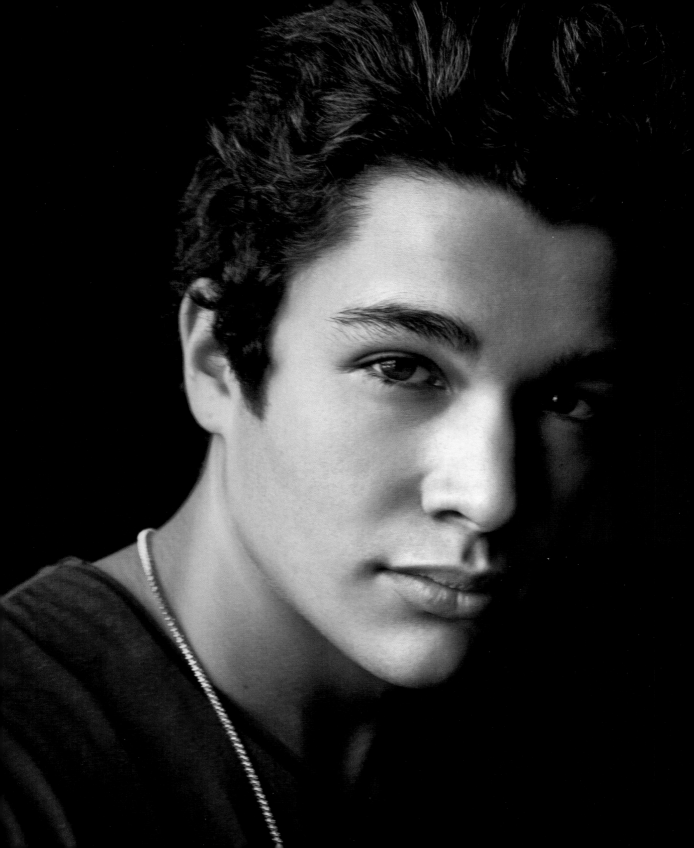

Although I was starting to figure out how YouTube worked and how to best shoot a video, I still had a lot to learn. Just take the first video I shot for the new Austin Mahone channel, a cover of Chris Brown's "With You," which I uploaded on January 14, 2011. My mom shot this one at our house in La Vernia. I'd already posted enough videos that we were always trying to think of new backgrounds and other ways to keep it interesting. So, for this one, we decided I should be walking down the hallway in our house while I was singing.

We cued the music on the stereo in the living room, my mom started filming me, and I started walking and singing. As I got farther down the hall, I was walking away from the music, so it was getting quieter. That did not sound good at all. My mom stopped filming, and we tried it again. And again. And again. Finally, we filmed it in pieces, turning up the stereo as I got farther away from it, and edited the sections together to create the whole song. But that's how it went

when Mom and I were doing all the jobs at once—artist, director, camera, sound. Or at least doing those jobs as best as we could.

I don't go back and watch these old videos that much anymore, but it's wild when I do, like stepping back in time—there I am with my braces on, and that puka shell necklace I wore every day, in our house in La Vernia, which we'd already started to pack up. The room you can see in the background in this video was our music room, where I kept my drums. But we'd already put them in storage by this point, because my mom and stepdad were getting divorced, and we were getting ready to sell the house and move back to San Antonio.

AC and I were still having fun doing stupid things for my new channel. Our first vlog on there, which we posted in February 2011, and is still online, was called "Potato and Radish." It ended with me and AC making the hand gesture for a heart, only to realize our attempts look more like vegetables than valentines. That still cracks me up.

It was hard to believe we'd only started all this six months earlier. My life was already changing FAST, and I had no idea then just how much—or how fast—things could and would continue to change. As 2011 progressed, and I spent more and more time on my new YouTube channel, I realized I actually had Mahomies. I was watching my audience grow every day, and I wanted to grow it more, so I got smarter about my approach.

At this point, I was posting a lot of covers, and I realized that if I posted a cover of a song that was ranked high on iTunes, a lot of people would be searching for it on YouTube. And when they searched for this song, my video might pop up right there along with the original version. I figured the more songs I covered, the more views I'd get. So that's what I did.

Once I started my own channel, I got my mom involved a lot more. I wanted the videos to look more professional (at least for me), so we started setting up lights and thinking about how and where we shot them.

I usually practiced a couple times before we started filming—getting down the lyrics and the moves—but that was about it. I've never been the fastest study, but for some reason, lyrics have always been easy for me. It's like once I hear a song it's all there in my head, forever. So it didn't take long for me to make a song my own in my videos.

Not that we didn't make plenty of mistakes. One time, my mom turned on the camera, and I started singing, until I realized the camera was shaking. I was like, *What is going on?* I was trying to stay focused and hit the next verse, but I had to look at my mom to see what was happening. She was laughing and couldn't stop.

"Mom, stop," I said.

She kept filming, shaking her head, like she was trying to pull it together.

"Mom, *stop*," I said again.

Finally, she stopped filming, and she stopped laughing. But then, as soon

"With You" Chris Brown cover - 14 yr old Austin Mahone with lyrics

as the camera went on again, she was laughing so hard and couldn't stop.

"I'm sorry," she said, shaking her head. "You're just so serious."

Of course I was serious! We were making a new video, and I wanted it to be good. "*Mom,*" I said.

"Sorry, you sound great," she said. "Let's do it again."

It took us like five or six takes to finally get through it because my mom kept laughing, but eventually she got over it.

Overall, we tried a lot of different things with the videos. We even did some in black and white, just to change it up a bit. And maybe I was serious in a lot of them… but it was all fun.

It felt like momentum was building in terms of the numbers of views and subscribers we were getting, but I had no idea what—if anything— that meant for me.

I was really starting to think of myself as a singer. People who watched my videos treated me like one. They weren't just telling me they liked my singing. They were also giving me tips about what I should sing and how I should use my voice, you know, trying to help me out. It was cool. I realized something was happening. *Maybe I can take this further,* I thought. So I

really dialed in, knowing if I kept working hard at it, and practiced
trained, that I would keep getting better and better.

Unbelievably, I wasn't the only person who thought this. Not long af
got my music channel up and running, it became clear that enough pe
were into what I was doing that I should offer them a way to connect with
directly. So my mom and I set up a PO box for fan mail, and I announced
address in a YouTube video. It was so wild the first time we found an envelo
addressed to me in what was definitely a girl's handwriting: my first fan lett
(Of course, we did a video of me opening it.) Not long after that, I starte
getting all sorts of amazing things in the mail—stuffed animals, hand-draw
posters, personal notes. I hung up every single piece of mail I got in my room
Girls I didn't even know had taken the time to write to me because they liked
my singing. It felt incredible.

And then, that winter, not long after I
started my channel, my mom got an e-mail
that changed everything.

See, this is what happened: When I
started my own channel, AC and I agreed
that I should go onto the channel we
started together and tell our subscribers
to come to my new channel. When that
happened, it made my new channel the
number one fastest-growing channel on
YouTube for that month.

Around the same time, this company was starting a new convention

called Playlist Live to showcase YouTube artists with fast-growing channels. They had noticed me and tracked down my mom to ask me to perform at it. Even though I'd quickly jumped to something like twenty or thirty thousand YouTube subscribers and about ten thousand Twitter followers, I couldn't believe anyone had noticed. Playlist Live helped us make our first piece of merch—a T-shirt with a picture of me on it. Selling shirts with my face on it was definitely weird, but also pretty cool at the same time.

The convention happened in March 2011. My mom, AC, and I flew down to Orlando, Florida, for it. Suddenly, after months of shooting videos in AC's bedroom and pretty much every room in my house, I found myself among the biggest YouTube stars. And there I was: Austin from La Vernia,

Sure, fifty people doesn't sound like a lot. But think about where I'd started.

Texas, and my little YouTube channel. Honestly, it was weird to be there with people who had MILLIONS of fans on YouTube when mostly no one knew who I was. And I had never really performed live before, except for those local talent shows.

I always say I don't get nervous. But I'll admit I was definitely a little on edge that day. I was going to be singing on this BIG stage for the first time, ever, and I didn't even have a set list. I just had my iPhone with the music for the covers I was going to sing. The sound person hooked it up to the soundboard, and that was it.

I was backstage, pacing a little, running through the songs in my mind, trying to remember all the little details I wanted to remember—not only the lyrics, but how I was going to move my hands at which different parts. And then they announced me:

"AUSTIN MAHONE."

I hit play, the music started, and that's when my nerves got the worst,

because it was like, *There's no going back now.* So I just went for it. I walked out onto the stage, feeling all those nerves inside me.

I knew there were several hundred people at the event walking around, but I didn't know if any of them would bother watching me. But as soon as I got out there, I saw that there were were maybe fifty girls at the front of the stage all waiting to watch me sing. And I remember thinking, *This is pretty cool.*

Sure, fifty people doesn't sound like a lot. But think about where I'd started. Here were fifty kids who'd gotten their parents to drive them to come watch me. When I thought about it that way, it was amazing. Suddenly, I didn't feel so nervous anymore. I felt like I belonged there onstage, and I had the best time singing the songs that were my favorite to perform back then: "With You," "I'll Be," and "Beautiful Soul."

That whole weekend was awesome. It was my first time meeting fans—well, other than those girls at the mall in San Antonio a few months earlier. And it felt crazy to have them want to take pictures with me. Again, I was still used to some people in school calling me names for singing the songs I did. So this was a whole new world on pretty much every level. I still see some of those early fans on Twitter, or run into them sometimes, and think back. I still remember and appreciate them. I mean, they really were the first people to believe in me (other than my mom, my family, and the guys, of course), and I will always be grateful to them for that.

Plus, I got to meet some cool YouTube artists who actually had whole careers where they traveled around playing for their fans. We all hung out, and it felt like maybe this could be my life in the not-too-distant future, too. The convention was at this big hotel, and there were all these kids my age running around, just having a good time. AC and I were in it together, just like we had been from the beginning, having fun.

Things started to move pretty quickly after that. School still wasn't great, but it was starting to feel like a small part of my life compared to all the other cool stuff that was happening. Playlist Live changed everything because my mom and I realized that I had real fans out there, and they wanted the chance to connect with me, however we were able to make that happen.

I started offering fans the chance to chat with me on Skype. That was cool because I got to see them one-on-one and maybe sing their favorite song, or have a conversation with them. Some girls were so nervous they were literally speechless, so I would just sing them a song. And sometimes they would start to cry. That really made an impression on me; it meant so much for them to get to spend time with me like that, and it meant a lot for me, too. So I tried to make the experience fun for them.

By this point, I was really working hard to be a singer, only I wasn't as good as I wanted to be. So I also used Skype to take lessons from a vocal coach I'd found in another city. She definitely taught me some basics I could work with for a while.

So even though everything wasn't perfect for me in La Vernia, I put all my focus into the things that were going well in my life—my singing, my YouTube channel, my family, AC and my other friends. Luckily, that's the great thing about singing: It makes me forget everything else while I'm doing it.

For many reasons, my mom and I were both relieved when she sold our house in La Vernia in the summer of 2011 and we were getting ready to move back to San Antonio. Everything was changing, and she sat me down to talk about it. That's one of the best things about my mom—she always talks through things with me. I appreciate that.

"If I have a regular full-time job, there's no way I can travel as much as you need to in order to grow your career," she said.

I just looked at her, not sure what she was getting at.

"All of this is still so new that I don't really have a concrete plan," she said.

I nodded my head. It did feel like it had all happened really fast.

"I don't know what's going to happen," she added. "But I'm thinking about quitting my job."

No way. My mom believed in me so much she was considering

I knew what a big deal it was, what my mom and my grandparents were doing for me, and I felt so lucky to have them.

quitting her job at a great company she had been with for years in order to travel with me and basically be my manager.

"Thank you, Mom," I said, really meaning it.

The only people who knew I was leaving were my boys—AC, Robert, Zach, and our other friend Cameron—and we'd already made a pact to visit each other all the time.

That whole summer was really busy because I was practicing my singing, recording new videos, Skyping with fans, and traveling for shows. Also, after Playlist Live, my online merch store started doing really well. I couldn't have been happier to be doing what I loved and connecting with more and more fans.

Everyone in my family was so amazing and supportive. Granddad and Mema let us move back in with them so Mom wouldn't have to worry about a mortgage payment or rent and our other expenses would be minimal. Their house was nice, but it was a little cramped with all of us there. Mom and I kept our clothes in big plastic bins in our bedrooms because we didn't have a lot of space. I knew what a big deal it was, what my mom and my grandparents were doing for me, and I felt so lucky to have them.

I was not exactly excited about starting at Johnson High School in San Antonio for my sophomore year, though. I would be the new kid again.

But I was not at all prepared for what happened during my first few days at my new school.

On my first day, I could actually hear people talking about me in the halls, saying things like, "Oh man, we've got a new kid."

I would rather they'd have just ignored me completely, but this wasn't so bad. And then, the next day, the things I overheard in the halls changed.

"That's that kid from YouTube."

"That's that Austin guy."

I tried to ignore them and keep walking, but one of them stepped in front of me. "Aren't you that kid on YouTube?" he said. "You sing?" But he wasn't asking in a nice way.

"Yeah, that's me," I said and kept it pushing to my next class.

And then I was in math class later that day, and when I turned around, this girl was taking pictures of me with her phone. It was really strange. I tried to concentrate on what the teacher was saying, but I felt self-conscious and it was hard to focus. Not long after that, I saw that the girl had posted

her photos of me on Twitter. And even though I've never been the most studious guy, I was like, *Man, it's really hard to concentrate with all of this going on. I can't even learn.*

The next day, these two girls pulled me out of class to interview me for a story in the school newspaper. Not only was I the new guy, but also everyone seemed to know who I was and have an opinion about it.

I lasted only two weeks.

I decided I wanted to finish high school from my room at my grandparents' house. I didn't care about going to football games. I didn't care about going to prom. I liked singing and wanted to concentrate on it more. I know that getting an education is important, and I felt that being homeschooled would give me more flexibility to concentrate on music. I knew what I wanted to do with my life.

Of course, this was a big decision. My mom literally cried over it for weeks because she was so worried about whether or not I had the discipline to do all the work basically on my own, and whether she had the dedication to be my teacher. Finally, she sat me down for another one of our serious conversations.

"I've been agonizing over this decision," she said. "I know it's the right thing to do."

"It'll be fine, Mom," I said. "It'll be great."

I WAS ONLY FIFTEEN YEARS OLD, BUT THIS WAS MY DREAM, AND I KNEW I HAD TO PURSUE IT.

"You know, homeschooling isn't easy," she said. "You've got to stay focused and stay productive."

"I will, Mom, I promise," I said.

Okay, I'll admit it—that was easier said than done. In my defense, though, it's hard to stay focused and productive when you're in your room. I was taking my classes online, so I'd do a question, and sometimes it would be really hard. So I'd sit there thinking, and then I'd be like, *I'm going to watch a quick YouTube video, you know, give my mind a break for a second.* Three hours later, I'd come back to the question, and it was still hard.

The biggest problem for me was I missed my friends. It was a forty-five-minute drive back to La Vernia, so I could only hang out with them on the weekends, and only when we could get one of our parents to drive us. I had no friends in San Antonio, so it could get pretty lonely. That part sucked.

The upside was that I had a lot more time to sing and post videos, so I was a lot more productive once I wasn't in regular school anymore. I'd get up, do my schoolwork, make videos, post them, and go to bed. I did that every day for a year, and now that my videos were being watched by millions of fans, I never felt alone. That's why I'm so devoted to you and I work so hard to make sure I get to come to your hometown and sing for you. You've gotten me through some really tough times.

By the fall, my mom had quit her job as a mortgage loan officer to manage me full-time.

"Okay, we're trying this for a year," she told me after she gave notice. "If nothing happens by that point, I'll probably have to go back and get a regular job again, and we may have to rethink all of this."

NOW THAT MY VIDEOS WERE BEING WATCHED BY MILLIONS OF FANS, I NEVER FELT ALONE.

"I totally get it," I said.

And I did. She was the best, and I was going to work hard to make her proud. I was a little nervous about it because I really didn't want to let her down. I was only fifteen years old, but this was my dream, and I knew I had to pursue it. And my mom did, too. So here we went.

But it wasn't like I had a career at this point. I had a YouTube channel with a bunch of videos on it and a few hundred thousand followers. When I posted a video, it now got anywhere from several hundred thousand to a million or even two million views. So that was definitely something. But I still didn't know where it could lead.

My mom started getting approached more often by the parents of girls who wanted to book me to fly to their hometowns and perform at their birthday parties, or do small club shows so they and their friends could come see me. I loved getting to meet my fans face-to-face, and that was always an adventure. My mom did an amazing job of keeping track of all of this, and taking care of our travel arrangements.

At the end of October, I performed at a birthday party outside Chicago for these two sisters who were both big fans and had, like, a hundred girls come out to see me play at their house. It was so much fun. Their family was so nice to us, and since they were some of our earliest supporters, we still always try to make sure they're able to come to my Chicago shows.

We'd traveled all the way there, so my mom and I decided to get the most out of our time in Chicago. Since I'd only been able to play at a

private party, we decided to post on Twitter that I was going to check out "The Bean" in Millennium Park, just to see if I had any fans in Chicago. Probably no one would be there, but if anyone did show up, I'd get to say hey and meet some fans.

As we were walking over to the park, we looked at my Twitter feed and saw some photos that had just been posted from there. It looked like a lot of girls were at the park, way more than we'd expected.

"You know what, it's Sunday, there's probably a lot of tourists in the park," my mom said. "I'm sure that's all it is."

Just to be sure, though, we decided that when we got to The Bean, we'd go up the side ramp, instead of the main steps, so we'd have a chance to check out what was going on before anyone really knew I was there. Only, as we got closer, a few girls who were leaning up against the ramp railing turned and saw me. They started screaming and running toward me. It was crazy. They were literally jumping over the railing. It looked like a mob, and it was coming right for me.

"Just keep moving," Mom said. "Don't stop, because if you do, we won't be able to start moving again."

We did our best to push through the crowd, but there were hundreds of girls there, and they were all screaming and trying to talk to me. Honestly, it got a little out of hand.

All of a sudden, these two big cops pushed toward us.

"Who are your handlers?" they said. "Who are you here with?"

"No one," Mom said. "It's just us."

Because there were so many girls there, they assumed I was there with an event organizer or PR person, and it took us a while to convince them we'd had no idea anything like that was going to happen. They brought us to a security building in the park and kept us there long enough for the crowd to thin out. Even then, they drove us back to our hotel in one of their unmarked cars via an underground garage so no one would see us leave and come after us.

"Do you know how many girls were out there?" an officer asked us.

We both shook our heads, still in a little bit of shock.

"There were about a thousand girls out there," he said.

A thousand girls? There to see me? That was wild.

On Halloween 2011, I got invited to perform at *Teen Hoot* in Nashville, which was superfun. I did a bunch of songs, including "Find Your Love" by Drake; a medley of "Never Let You Go" and "Let Me Love You;" and "I'll Be," which was becoming kind of a signature song for me at that point. When I got interviewed as part of their online coverage, I even sang a bit for the interviewer. And that's where I got my ukulele.

Best of all, I met this really cool female singer there named Alyssa Shouse, who was another big YouTube artist. We totally hit it off and realized we liked to sing the same kind of songs. So we decided to do a duet of "No Air," which was originally recorded by Jordin Sparks and Chris Brown. The idea was we'd each record our part, and then we'd have a couple friends I'd met through YouTube, who were good at this stuff, edit the separate sections together into one video we could post online for our fans.

We didn't have the best camera at the time, and we wanted it to be in HD so it would look more professional. So when my mom and I got home

Mistletoe - Justin Bieber - music video cover by Austin Mahone -

Mistletoe - Justin Bieber - music video cover by Austin Mahone -

and went to film my part, we decided to shoot it using the camera on my laptop. Only, when my mom was holding up my computer with the camera facing me, she couldn't see if she was getting me in the shot or not. I could see everything. And sometimes I was out of the frame. So I had to keep telling her to move the camera over so that she was actually getting footage of me. It took many, many takes. That definitely would have made for a good behind-the-scenes video. But, luckily, the video turned out great, and made a big impact, not only because it was my first duet, but also because it exposed me to a lot of Alyssa's fans, too, which was cool. Not to mention, it was our first video that we tried to make look legit, and I think we mostly pulled it off.

By November 2011, it really felt like things were happening, even though we were still a two-person operation running things out of Granddad and Mema's

house. A few local TV stations had interviewed me, which was cool. We'd gotten a new camera, and I did a cover of Justin Bieber's "Mistletoe," which went viral. It was definitely a step up from all my earlier videos, production-wise. I was starting to get so much fan mail that Mema took over handling it. She helped me hang up all the posters and drawings I got in my bedroom, and soon, my entire room—all four walls *and* the ceiling—was totally plastered in fan art. It looked great.

Throughout that fall, I traveled a bunch to play birthday parties. And we booked some more shows. One of my first big performances was for about four hundred of my fans at a teen club in Houston. Not only was that the most people I'd ever performed for, but it also got some press coverage. My nana and aunt Robin came out, which helped make it a really special night for me. They even helped run the merch table. (Logan and Rylie weren't there for this one—Logan wasn't even a year old yet—but they come to see my shows now whenever possible.)

When it was time to take the stage, though, I saw that it was so small, literally like a couch flipped upside down. So, basically, imagine me standing on a small piece of furniture, singing my heart out for four hundred people. I couldn't move around while I performed. I couldn't even take a step.

But I put everything into my singing, and it felt so cool to be performing my first big show. In fact, I performed my first TWO big shows because we sold out the first night so quickly that they let us come back the next night and do it all again for another four hundred people. There were eight hundred people who wanted to see me sing?! I couldn't believe it.

Just like with the videos, the more shows I did, the bigger it became. It all just got better and better.

That December, I got to go back to New York City, much sooner than I'd thought I would considering the warning Granddad had given me during our first trip just the previous summer. My mom had always wanted to go, too, and this was her first time, so it felt pretty cool to be able to make that happen for her. We had booked a show at a club called DROM, and it sold out so quickly that we booked a second show for the same day. It sold out, too. My cousin Mac was the MC, and we had so much fun.

Around this time, I posted a new video, a cover of Adele's "Someone Like You," and it became my first video to score ten million views. The year my mom set for giving this whole thing a try was about half over. It was all happening.

But, as January wore on, we stopped getting calls and e-mails about playing shows. People my mom had met in the music business warned her that January is always slow and we shouldn't get antsy. But we'd given up everything—my school, her job—and it was hard not to worry it might not happen after all.

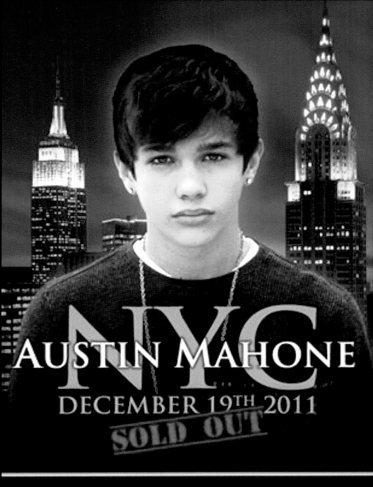

At this point, it was just me and Mom in it together, doing everything we could for my music. That's how my fans came to know her and call her Mama, or Mama Mahone, which is a nickname she came up with when she was tagging an online photo of herself with AC and me at the first Playlist Live back in 2011.

The fans really started to recognize her—following her on Twitter and Instagram, and asking to have their photos taken with her when we were out at a performance or event. After that, she'd pop up on my Ustream from time to time, just to say hi, and she's sort of been everyone's mom ever since.

We'd had a slow winter—like, scary slow—but luckily we had a cool project to keep us busy. My mom has always loved Nashville. She's kind of country at heart. So we went there a lot, and around then, she met this lady who managed a band. They'd written a song five years earlier that they'd never recorded, and they felt like they

were too old for the material now, so they were just sitting on the song. Meanwhile, I was tired of singing nothing but covers, and I wanted to record and perform an original song for once. They offered to give me the song, which was really cool of them, and I jumped on the opportunity.

The best part was I got to go to Nashville for the recording session. Ever since I'd left high school the previous fall, I'd spent almost every day in my room, trying to get through my schoolwork and recording videos. My friends were all back in La Vernia, and I barely went anywhere or saw anyone. So it felt amazing to get out and go to a different state and do something new and exciting.

The space where we were recording was in a room at the producer's house. It was the first studio I'd ever been in, with real microphones and all these weird machines that were like nothing I'd ever seen before. Once we got started, singing felt just like what I was used to by that point—well, except for it sounded a lot better than when I was recording myself. Before I knew it, I'd recorded my first single, "11:11."

That whole trip was amazing. Here I was, traveling, recording my first single. And then, while we were there, I was in this coffee shop in Nashville when I looked up and saw this really tall, pretty girl who looked kind of familiar to me. It couldn't be. Only, yeah, it was: Taylor Swift. I had to go say hi to her. I walked up to her table, feeling kind of shy and dorky, but she looked up and gave me a big smile.

"Are you Taylor?" I said.

"Yeah," she said.

"Hey, my name's Austin Mahone," I said. "I'm a singer on YouTube."

Her smile got even bigger.

"That's really cute," she said. "Keep up the hard work and never stop believing."

"Thanks," I said. "Do you mind if I get a picture with you?"

"Of course not," she said.

We posed together and my mom took the picture. Little did I know at the time that we'd meet again a year later, under circumstances I couldn't have imagined then. Life is too crazy sometimes.

Once we got the track down, we wanted to find the right way to put "11:11" out. So we decided to release it on iTunes on Valentine's Day, and I would play a show to celebrate, where I'd perform "11:11" for the first time. I still felt bad that I'd never been able to meet all those girls who'd come out to see me in Chicago the previous fall, and we'd always wanted to do something just for them. So we decided to book my first-ever single release show at a theater just outside Chicago.

We were really busy in February, pulling everything together for the single release and the show, and things had also picked up again, just like all those music industry people had promised my mom they would. The phone started ringing, and people started hitting me up on YouTube and Facebook. Two major labels had expressed interest in signing me, and one of their A&R guys was even planning to come out to my Chicago show to see me sing and tell me what his label had to offer.

Even though a lot of way bigger stuff has happened since then, that was probably one of the best nights of my life. The show was great. It was packed, and everyone in the audience was so into it and really excited about my new song. With a major label A&R rep in the audience, it felt like things were taking off for me. And that was before my single even dropped.

After the show, I went back to my hotel room. And then, right at midnight, at the moment when my song was actually released, I went to the iTunes store, and there it was: my first song. It was crazy, pressing play on my own song and hearing my own voice on iTunes. Definitely one of those moments I'll always remember.

We ended up getting interest from a total of three major labels and a few indie labels, plus seven or eight different managers who were all

THAT WAS A HUGE MOMENT, LIKE, WOW, WE REALLY DID IT—THIS IS ACTUALLY HAPPENING.

excited by the momentum I'd been able to create on YouTube and social media, without the help of anyone but my mom (and AC, of course). That was a huge moment, like, *Wow, we really did it—this is actually happening.*

My mom and I took trips to Los Angeles and Nashville to meet with potential managers and see what they could bring to the table. And we went to New York City for meetings with the record labels, too. I couldn't wait to get something—anything—started, and I was ready to sign as soon as possible and start making more music. But my mom cautioned me that whatever decision we made now, we'd be locked into for years, so we should take our time and make sure it was the right fit for me. I knew she was right, but it was frustrating. At least it was fun to travel and meet new people. And

of course it was exciting to have the music industry suddenly take me seriously. I tried to be patient, even though I'm not the most patient person.

In February 2012, Rocco started reaching out to everyone he could to find me. He e-mailed all my friends, my mom, and even my old school. My mom finally called him back, and they started talking. He explained that he had been following me for months, watching all my YouTube videos and socials. It was the cover of Drake's "Shot for Me" that caused him to reach out. We talked for a while before my mom and I agreed to meet the Chase team. When we met, Rocco and his partners told us how impressed they were and that they wanted to take me to the next level. They were amazed that it was just me and my mom shooting all these videos and posting everything.

All the hard work we had been doing was starting to pay off.

In the middle of all this, I got the best news when I was invited back to perform at Playlist Live, only this time I was one of the main attractions with thousands of fans there to see me. It was wild to see how much had changed for me in only one year. At my first Playlist Live, it had all been such a new experience. It was cool, but I didn't

At this point, it was just me and Mom in it together, doing everything we could for my music.

feel like I knew what was going on, and there were definitely moments when I'd felt a little shy.

The second year was a totally different story. AC and I both felt a lot more confident, and that made the whole thing even more fun. Plus, Robert

came with us, too. Not only that, but also so many more people who were attending that year knew who we were and wanted to stop and say hi and get their picture taken with us.

As soon as we walked into the hotel ballroom for the pre-party, I knew it would be a good time. I recognized people I'd hung out with the year before and got to meet so many new people. There was a dance floor, and the next thing I knew, Robert and I were dancing in the middle of a circle, doing our thing while everyone danced and clapped around us. We had a blast. It felt amazing to perform the next day, now that I'd done a few shows and learned a couple things. And I felt ready for everything that was coming next.

In late March, the guys from Chase flew us down to Miami to meet everyone in their camp and see what they were all about. They sent a limo to pick us up from the airport, and they put us up at a beautiful hotel in South Beach, all of which was really cool. But my mom always warned me that we shouldn't have our judgment clouded by that kind of stuff, which was everywhere in the music industry. Still, it felt so amazing to be sitting in the back of this big stretch limo, getting zipped along the highway, with the beach, the palm trees, and the big fancy hotels on the horizon.

And all of this was happening because AC and I recorded some videos and posted them on YouTube, and I'd never stopped believing, even when there was no obvious reason to believe.

It was the best feeling in the world. Plus, I never felt like we had to be

All of this was happening because AC and I recorded some videos and posted them on YouTube, and I'd never stopped believing, even when there was no obvious reason to believe.

on guard with the guys from Chase. They just wanted to make sure we were taken care of and felt welcomed, and we did. I started to relax and enjoy myself.

One of the things I noticed about them was that they'd been friends for a long time, and they often seemed to know one another's thoughts without ever having to say anything. That reminded me of my friendship with AC, Robert, and Zach, and it made me feel comfortable around them, like maybe we were kind of the same in some way.

The four partners at Chase were members of a team who all shared the responsibility, but at the same time, everyone had their own way of communicating and their own area of expertise. Together they formed a well-oiled machine. And they were fun. Hanging out with them in Miami, I started to feel like this could be my life now.

My mom and I were already leaning toward signing with them for a lot of important reasons—they'd been in the business for a long time and managed very successful artists. Even though they were more in the hip-hop and R&B world, and I knew I was probably going to be more of a pop singer, my mom and I could tell they knew a lot of people and had the right hookups.

On our last night in Miami, they dropped us back at our hotel. I walked into our hotel room first, with my mom behind me. I walked up to the

I STARTED TO FEEL LIKE THIS COULD BE MY LIFE NOW.

window, and it was like I just knew what I needed to do. I turned around and looked at my mom.

"Mom, they're the ones," I said.

"Austin, I was just getting ready to say the same exact thing. I just feel like these are the right guys."

We were pretty much decided, but we weren't ready to make it definite yet.

O n April 4, 2012, I turned sixteen. The day before my birthday, we had a family dinner to celebrate. But for my actual birthday, I wanted to do something special and knew exactly what it was going to be.

Now, part of the conversation with the guys from Chase had been the idea that if I signed with them, I was going to move to Miami for at least six months so they could help develop me as an artist. I had lived in Texas my whole life. It was all I knew. And all my friends and family were there. But I knew I had to give Miami a try. I wanted to get there and start working right away. But my mom said we couldn't leave yet. There was too much happening, and it was all happening at once. I knew there was a good chance I was about to leave for Miami, though, and I wanted to do something cool for the friends who'd supported me from the beginning.

I had my mom rent us a white stretch Hummer limo. It was a Friday afternoon, and I picked up AC, Robert, and Zach at

school and brought them back to San Antonio for the night. We went bowling, saw a movie, and had dinner at Olive Garden. I felt like I was leaving Texas on a good note, and my boys knew that I'd always appreciate them, and that we're going through this adventure together. I was MORE than ready to go live my dream.

The guys at Chase invited us down for a second visit in mid-April to spend five days in Miami and talk about what it would be like to work together. During this trip, they took me into a real studio for the first time. Everyone likes to tease me about how I was like a deer in headlights when we stepped inside. And when I saw the console with its thousands of knobs and buttons—so many ways to improve the sound of a song, which were all totally new to me—I did have this feeling like: *What am I doing here?*

The guys messed with me a little bit, but I was starting to get that that was just the way they were. I immediately felt right at home with them—I felt like I was with older versions of my friends.

Rocco clapped me on the back and led me up to the producer's chair.

"Come on, I'll show you around," he said.

Rocco gave me a mini-lesson on how everything worked. And I knew I

When I heard "Say Somethin," I knew it was the song for me. We all did.

was right where I belonged, which was really cool after my mom and I had taken so many leaps of faith to get there.

We didn't want to lose any of the momentum I'd built in the past year, so I was beyond ready to put out my next single ASAP. And they wanted me to get a sense of what it would be like to work with them, so we decided we should try recording a song or two while I was there.

The big question was what sound I should go for. Since I was still developing as an artist, it made sense to try a few different approaches and see what felt right to me when I was singing and performing, and of course, what my fans responded to the most. The guys played a few different songs for me, and I listened to them all closely. This was a big decision. When I heard "Say Somethin," I knew it was the song for me. We all did. It had a good, fun feel, and it sounded like me. We all felt like it could be big. Plus, it just felt good when I sang it, which is always the most important. And even though my sound has evolved a lot since then, that song is still an important part of my live show.

The guys brought in Maejor Ali and Mike Posner, two really talented producers and songwriters, to work with me. Maejor has worked with everyone from Iggy Azalea to Ne-Yo, and Mike has done songs with everyone from Pharrell to Maroon 5, and on and on for both of these guys.

When I walked into the studio to work with them on the first day, I was definitely like, *Wow, how's this gonna go?* But both guys were easy to work with, and Maejor was great about coaching me and helping me. I settled in really quick. In fact, it didn't take long for the studio to become one of my favorite places to be. And as soon as my mom left the room (I don't know why, but it always makes me uncomfortable when she's watching

me record—I guess it's just a mom thing), I powered through all the songs we wanted to cut. "Say Somethin" was the obvious next single. It felt amazing to walk out of there knowing I'd nailed it.

It was also a good chance to see what the guys from Chase were all about. I guess you could say I got a good read on the four of them during that second visit, and that's what cemented my decision for me. It was so easy to be around them, and I felt like I trusted each and every one of them already when it came to the decisions I was facing at that point in my career.

My mom and I let them know we were ready to sign a management deal with them. That meant putting talks with the record labels on hold, which felt a little weird, since I couldn't wait to put out more music. But the guys promised me that I wasn't going to regret this. And they were right. Better opportunities were just around the corner, even though I had no idea what was coming for me.

The last week of April, I also had my confirmation through the Catholic church. And I got my braces off, which was another one of the best days of my life. I'd fought my mom hard about getting braces, but my teeth had been so bad that I really didn't have a choice. And then I'd had to endure them for two and a half years, much of which I spent in front of a camera. But, finally, I was getting them off, six months early, and I couldn't have been happier to be done with them.

I really knew I'd made the right decision about my management team when they flew down to San Antonio for my confirmation. That meant a lot

to me. Even better, the next day, they all came over to Granddad and Mema's house, and we signed the deal right there, right where it started for this to even be possible: my bedroom. I can't even tell you how amazing that felt, standing there in my room, where I'd spent so many hours alone—lonely and bored and wondering if it was ever going to happen for me, or if those kids at school were right and all my YouTube stuff was really stupid—and now it was the exact same spot where all my dreams were coming true.

I looked over at my mom and thought about how she'd always been there for me, and the big risk she'd taken by quitting her job and giving me a year to do something with my music. And I looked around at the guys from Chase Entertainment—who all believed in me so much, and who already felt like the big brothers I'd never had. It was an intense moment for me in that room right there.

It was so crazy, too, because when I'd first started out, I'd never in a million years thought I'd ever be signing with a real management company and traveling all over, singing for real fans. And now, everything that was happening was so much better than I'd even dared to imagine. And it was just the beginning.

There was so much good stuff happening right then. And that's what I tried to focus on. Sometimes it was rough, though, because there were also some really hard moments during that year. Earlier that winter, it seemed like everyone in my family had allergies and was always sneezing and coughing. But after a few weeks, we all got better. Except for Mema. It seemed like her cough was only getting worse. Finally, she went to the doctor and found out she had lung cancer, and she never even smoked. That was so scary and awful.

Around the same time, my dog, Angel, who I had since I was five, got really sick and was in and out of the hospital. We didn't know how we'd be able to take care of her, or if she'd even be able to move with us. Finally, the vet told us there was nothing more we could do for her and that she was suffering. We were with Angel when he put her down. She'd always been there, looking out for me, and it was really sad to not have her with us anymore.

Even with the difficult stuff that was happening, life didn't slow down at all. In fact, it sped up, if that was even possible. A little more than a month after my sixteenth birthday, on May 12, my mom and I officially moved

EVERYTHING THAT WAS HAPPENING WAS SO MUCH BETTER THAN I'D EVEN DARED TO IMAGINE. AND IT WAS JUST THE BEGINNING.

into our new condo, right on the beach in Miami. She'd only signed a six-month lease because she was still thinking it might be better for us to be based out of San Antonio—it was familiar to us, and we'd soon be traveling so much for my career. But by the end of the first month, we both knew moving to Miami was the best thing we could have done. And personally, I loved Miami and was happy we were staying for a while.

I don't think things could have happened any faster than they did. Within my first week in Miami, we did a photo shoot and started working on choreography for the Q102 Springle Ball show I had coming up in Philadelphia. This was something already in the works, and it was a big deal. The radio station nominated me for its Next Big Thing contest leading up to the show, and the listeners had chosen me as the winner. Past winners included Lady Gaga and Katy Perry. I'd be performing with Enrique Iglesias and Flo Rida (who I had no clue I would be collaborating with months later) in front of twenty thousand people. I had some serious rehearsing to do.

Before I knew it, the day of the Springle Ball show had arrived. They had two stages, and I was on the smaller one, which could barely hold three people, making it really challenging for my dancers and me, but I was *there*. It was my first time performing in a packed arena, and everyone was screaming and dancing and having a great

I DON'T THINK THINGS COULD HAVE HAPPENED ANY FASTER THAN THEY DID.

time. It was amazing. I'm always going to remember that feeling—it wa[s] like the ultimate rush of energy. My show was pretty simple at that point— four backup dancers wearing blue jeans and white T-shirts—but we sti[ll] use some of the choreography from back then, and it just felt differen[t] somehow to have a crew with me onstage, like I was a real performer.

All of this was cool, but what I really wanted to focus on was getting som[e] new songs out to my fans as soon as possible. I dropped "Say Somethin" o[n] June 5, 2012, and as soon as it went up on iTunes, we promoted it as har[d] as possible. It was the first release with my new management team and w[e] released it independently (meaning without the push of a major recor[d] label). It did really well on iTunes and reached #34 on *Billboard's* Top 4[0] chart. It definitely got a lot of people's attention and helped me to kick of[f] what I wanted to do as an artist.

It was also immediately clear that plenty of people beyond the YouTube world were like, *Who's this random kid who's putting out songs?* Our goal was to get me, and my music, out *everywhere* in the world so that everyone in the world would know who that random kid was.

From there, it all just started to roll. I had another big first a week later when I was in Chicago, performing at the B96 Pepsi Summer Bash on June 16. It was cool because I was getting to know some of the people I was sharing a stage with—like Mike Posner and Flo Rida for starters—so it was beginning to feel like this was my world, too. Not to mention, Toyota Park held thirty thousand people; things kept getting bigger and better. My set was short but fun, and I was feeling good coming offstage.

And then I got into the car to head back to our hotel, and when the driver turned on the engine, there it was: my single "Say Somethin" coming out of the car speakers, being played on the radio, just at that exact moment. It was my first time ever hearing myself on radio, and it was almost overwhelming. *This is weird,* I thought. *This is so cool. But this is just strange.* It's like, I was living this new life every day, but it was still hard to believe it was *my life.*

That summer was going by fast, and we had a really important show coming up right after that at the Best Buy Theater in New York City. The show wasn't huge in terms of capacity (the theater holds twenty-two hundred people, which was small compared to the past couple radio shows), but it was *big* because it was my show and it sold out in minutes! And it was promoted just on Twitter, which is even more amazing. So that was really cool, too, for you guys to support me like that. It was also a showcase for me as we were shopping my record deal. Most of the time artists will showcase

SO WHAT STARTED AS A DANCE AUDITION LED INTO JOSH PLAYING A REAL LEADERSHIP ROLE IN MY CAMP—AND A FRIENDSHIP.

in the label's conference room, but that's boring. We wanted the labels to see a real Austin Mahone show and feel the energy in the building.

I was planning to do an hour set, which was a lot of material to get ready. Luckily for me, I met someone who has become one of the most important parts of my traveling family, and honestly, like a big brother to me: my dancer Josh Smith, who is now kind of like my dance captain. He came in for an audition with a whole group of dancers when we were getting this show ready, but there was just something I noticed about him right away. Not only is he an incredibly talented dancer—he and his crew had danced on *America's Best Dance Crew*—but also, he's got this quiet power to him or something. I don't even know how to describe it.

But he couldn't have come into my life at a better time. These were my first attempts to incorporate dance into my show, and honestly, I was a terrible dancer back then. I had never danced really. I was stiff and self-conscious and I had to learn everything. I soon realized that Josh wasn't just a great dancer, but he was also a really good teacher. He taught me so much, giving me tips on different pockets to hit when I'm performing live onstage—you know, how I could stop and stand in a certain spot for a couple seconds and connect with the audience before going on to the next move.

So what started as a dance audition led into Josh playing a real leadership role in my camp, and a friendship. It was also kind of a lonely time for me, so I was glad to have a new friend who was as passionate about performing as I was. Of course I was psyched to have my mom and my managers

I was living this new life every day, but it was still hard to believe it was my life.

around me all the time, but they were all adults. My crew was far away, back in La Vernia, finishing high school, and sometimes I got bored. So I was lucky to find Josh when I did.

But that didn't make rehearsals any easier. We were sweating for days and days (and days) going into that Best Buy show. I wanted everything to be perfect for my fans as well as the labels. And it worked! I signed my record deal the following month.

I wanted to do something really nice for my mom. Her dream car was a red Mustang convertible, so I decided to buy her one. Unfortunately, I couldn't surprise her because I was too young to buy a car on my own. But it still felt good.

She's always been there for me. She's really the best mom ever. Once I had her taken care of, I did get something for myself—a red Range Rover.

I got to see my crew in early August under circumstances that were about as cool as they could be. I was scheduled to shoot my video for "Say Somethin" (my first real music video) and we decided to set it at a high school with me dancing and singing with a bunch of other students. There was no question who would play my best friends, so we flew in AC, Robert, and Zach for the shoot.

The video was recorded at a private school in Hollywood, Florida, and we had so much fun doing it. It was another moment of being so happy with life and the way my career was progressing.

The rest of the year was busy with performing and recording and settling into my new life in Miami (at least for the little bit that I was there). Most of it was really, really good. But that September, I also went through one of the hardest things I've ever experienced so far. The one downside of moving to Miami was that we were suddenly far away from Granddad and Mema, just when Mema was beginning her cancer treatment.

Mom checked in with them all the time, and we did the best we could to see them as much as possible. I was busy with performances and appearances that couldn't be rescheduled, so we couldn't see her as much as we wanted to. People were starting to depend on me professionally, so personal time became basically nonexistent. But then we got word that Mema's cancer treatment wasn't going well and she was getting worse, fast.

So we flew to San Antonio…knowing it might be time for us to say good-bye without saying good-bye, if that makes any sense. It was really hard to walk into the room and see Mema looking so sick. But I was so glad to get that time to be with her, even though it was sad. My mema was always there for me, and I just wanted to be there for her. After visiting for a few days, we had to get back on the road. Mema understood—and supported me like she always had, which meant so much to me. It was the worst feeling saying good-bye to her because I knew I might never see her again. She had always done so much for me and cared for me. She was fun and funny and was pretty much the coolest grandma ever.

A few weeks later, Mema's condition got even worse and she was moved to hospice care. I couldn't go see her right away, so I recorded a video for my mom to play for her.

I didn't know exactly what I wanted say. But I took a deep breath and just started talking. "Hi Mema, it's Austin. I just want to tell you that I love you very much and I miss you. I'm so fortunate and thankful that you've been in my life. You're the best mema a boy could ever have. Thank you for always being there for me. I love you so much."

I was really, really sad, so I threw myself into work, which helped me keep my mind distracted a little, although of course I was thinking about her all the time. A couple days later, my mom called me from San Antonio to tell me that Mema had passed. It felt like the sky had fallen on me. Even when you know it's going to happen, you still can't prepare yourself for when it does. But that moment reminded me again that I have the best fans in the world.

So many people knew Mema because she'd been in some of my videos and she'd handled the fan mail. When I posted online that she'd passed away, we got the most amazing outpouring of love and support. It really meant so much to me, and to my mom, too, and it helped me to get through those first few months, which were the toughest.

That Thanksgiving, we all knew it was going to be sad to have dinner without Mema and her golden braid bread and all her wonderful cooking. So it was cool when Mike Blumstein invited us over to his house. He has a big family in Miami, and he insisted that we spend the holiday with them. Granddad and Aunt Lisa even flew in from San Antonio. It wasn't the same. But we made it the best we could given the circumstances, and I knew I had a lot to be thankful for.

Fortunately, after all that, the year ended on a better note. I got invited to be part of the Jingle Ball radio tour in December, which always includes some major acts, and that year it featured Enrique Iglesias, Ed Sheeran, and my old friend from Nashville, Taylor Swift.

I was singing for thousands of people every night, many of whom had never heard of me or my music before, so I was excited to have the chance to perform for them and hopefully turn them into Mahomies.

It felt like all my hard work was paying off. But I never wanted to forget where I'd come from, or how amazing any of this was. So I developed a ritual on that tour that has stayed with me to this day. The first time I played a Jingle Ball show, when I got there early for my sound check, I walked out into this huge, empty arena that would be filled with thousands of screaming fans in a few hours. I went all the way back toward the farthest row, climbed up to the top, and sat down. I took a picture of the view and thought: *Wow, this is a huge place. One day, I hope to be able to sell this out by myself.*

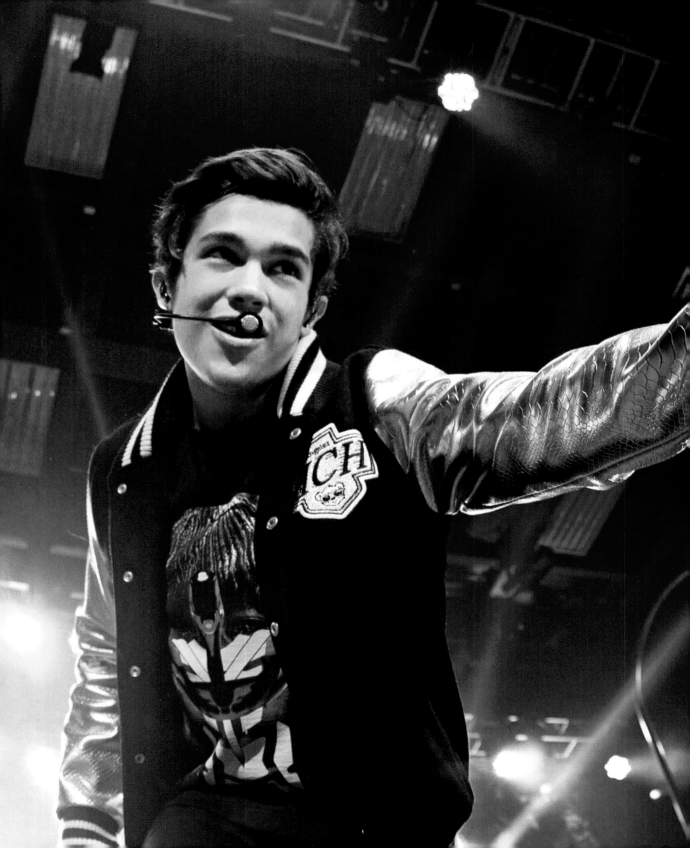

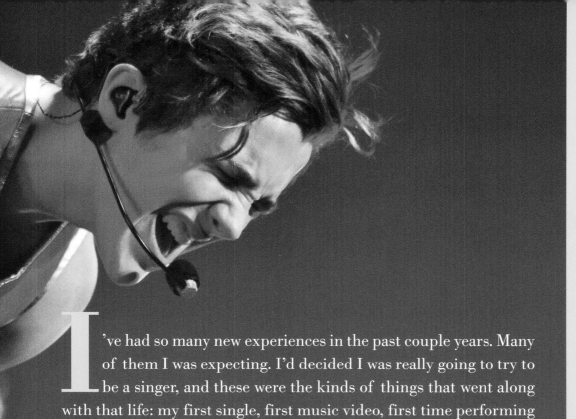

I've had so many new experiences in the past couple years. Many of them I was expecting. I'd decided I was really going to try to be a singer, and these were the kinds of things that went along with that life: my first single, first music video, first time performing for a packed arena. But there are some moments I don't think you can ever predict, the kind where you can't really believe it's happening the whole time it's happening. That would definitely be the best way to describe the once-in-a-lifetime opportunity I had on Sunday, March 31, 2013.

It was the annual Easter Egg Roll at the White House, and I had been invited to perform. I wasn't sure if we'd get to meet the First Family, and I figured even if we didn't, it would still be a day I'd remember forever. And then we were actually asked to go back and meet them. Just imagine how many people want to hang with the president of the United States of America.

The line was moving so slowly that it was looking like I wasn't going to get to meet the president after all because I needed to go get ready to perform. I was pretty disappointed. And then I was brought to the front so I could run off afterward and sing for everyone. I could hardly believe it. I got a picture with the president, his family, and my mom. He and his entire family were all so nice.

I went back into the studio in April to do a bunch of new songs. I was improving as a performer and learning how to handle myself in front of bigger crowds. But what I really cared about was defining my sound—finding the particular song or songs that would become my trademark and launch me from being that kid from YouTube to a respected world-class pop star. But finding—or writing—just the right song is one of the hardest things in music.

You've really got to choose your songs carefully. Telling if a song is right is something you feel in your gut. When you hear a song you love, you just love it. And you know: It's a hit. I definitely want to make music like that, music that makes people feel good, music that people love.

But when you make a song, it can be really hard to tell what you have after a while. You

TELLING IF A SONG IS RIGHT IS SOMETHING YOU FEEL IN YOUR GUT.

put your heart and soul into every recording, making it something you truly love, but then it gets played so many times in the studio that you get used to listening to it and it's like you can't really hear it anymore. You might be like, *Oh man, this song's crazy.* And then you play it for your friends, and they're like, *No way, man. It's not that good.*

I've learned you have to trust other people's ears at a certain point. After I've gotten my managers' feedback, I play it for my mom. And then I play it for the label. I play it for my dancers. I play it for my friends. And, always, I play it for AC. He's my harshest critic, which has nothing to do with being critical or mean. It's actually a great quality to have in a best friend, because he'll always tell me like it is. And I'd rather he be the one to keep it real than to have my fans or critics do it once the song is released. All I want from people is their honest opinions, and I consider all of them.

I've actually invited a lot of fans into the studio to give me their opinions, too. We did that during my recording session in April 2013 because we'd recorded a bunch of songs, and I couldn't decide which one should be

the next single. That recording session was with producer RedOne, who's worked with everyone from Lady Gaga to Enrique Iglesias to Nicki Minaj. We recorded a handful of songs and we were torn. They were all good, and I couldn't decide which one was my favorite and should be the next single.

When we were recording, there was a great group of fans hanging around outside the studio. It was late on one of the final nights of my sessions with Red. So we decided that we should bring these girls in, play the new material for them, and see what they thought. After all, the songs were really for them—the fans—more than anyone else.

Rocco and my security guard Joe brought me outside. It was really fun because no one was expecting what we were about to do.

"Hey, how's it going?" I said.

"Austin, can I get a picture?" one of the girls asked.

"Sure," I said. "But first, will you girls help me with something?"

So we led everyone into the studio and explained the situation. "Okay, we've got five new songs we're going to play for you tonight," I said. The girls got really excited when they heard that. They were not expecting this!

"We're not going to tell you what any of them are called," I continued. "Instead, we're going to give them each a number from one to five. And we want you to pick the one you like best."

So I played them all five songs.

And their favorite was the song that became my next single, "What About Love." We released it on June 10, 2013, and it became one of the central songs in the set I was performing that summer.

For that song, we were going for a Backstreet Boys/*NSYNC kind of feel because we thought it would be cool to bring back that classic nineties

pop sound. That song did better than my earlier singles, climbing to number 18 on the Top 40 chart. I was excited to be achieving one of my goals of reaching a wider audience.

I got some help reaching that goal during the summer of 2013 when I was asked to be the opening act for a *huge* artist I really admired, which was exactly the kind of opportunity I'd been hoping for. I have to tell you, though, when my managers told me who I'd be opening for, I couldn't believe it: Taylor Swift—who I'd always felt a real respect for, especially

Her bond with her fans is exactly what I always go for—she's not just up there performing; she's connecting, too.

since she'd been so nice to me back in Nashville. Plus, I admire how she's grown her career and respect her talent.

The first time we met backstage, I had to tell her where and how we'd met before. Of course, this time she knew I was a singer because I was her opener, and she smiled at me even bigger than before.

"Hey, Taylor, we actually met once in Nashville a couple years ago," I said. "I came up to you in a coffee shop and told you I was a singer on YouTube."

"I totally remember you," she said, laughing.

"No way," I said.

"No, I totally do."

I wasn't sure I believed her. But it didn't matter. I was her support act on a lot of her dates that summer, and we always got

I REALIZED I NEEDED A CHANGE. I DIDN'T LIKE BEING ALONE ALL THE TIME.

along well. Plus, I got to meet and hang a little with Ed Sheeran, who was also on the tour. He's a cool guy and very talented. That tour was fun and amazing, and I learned so much from watching Taylor. She's always such a pro.

Sure, I'd played big arenas during Jingle Ball. But this was different. These were stadiums. And the fans were so excited to see Taylor that it gave the shows this extra intensity. Her bond with her fans is exactly what I always go for—she's not just up there performing; she's connecting, too. Plus, there were more people there to see me than ever before, which was really cool.

It was also fun to be traveling with someone who was close to my own age, even though we were both so busy that we only bumped into each other here and there backstage. That's when it really hit me how lonely I'd been since moving to Miami the year before. Even though I'd been on the road a lot, I'd basically been there for a year and a half by myself. And this was after I'd spent basically a year at home alone in my bedroom at Granddad and Mema's when I was starting out.

I realized I needed a change. I didn't like being alone all the time. I had

my mom and my crew, but I needed something else. It was actually at the first show of the Taylor Swift tour that I finally did something about it. Mike Blumstein was on the road with me. We were killing time backstage when I discussed it with him.

"I need some friends to hang out with," I said. "It's all adults. I'm bored."

As I waited to hear what he'd have to say, I was nervous he'd think I wasn't serious enough about my music or that I wasn't working hard enough. But he just smiled at me.

"Why don't you fly your friends out here and have them roll with us?" he said.

Wow. Great idea. Could I really do that? I decided to try. I knew it might not be that easy, though, so I set all of it in motion as quickly as possible.

First, Robert and Zach came out on the road the summer before their senior year of high school. That was the best. We had a blast. The road became a much less lonely place for me. They decided they wanted to move to Miami, too. My mom talked to their moms, and they started making plans to finish high school early. It was a really busy time for me, so the plan was they'd help out, not just hang out. They were totally into that. Just like AC, they've always been so supportive of me.

And then AC moved in with us in July. We had an extra room in the condo, so it was perfect. Of course, by that point, I rarely had time to be in Miami, so AC joined me in my new home: on the road. All in all, it took about a year to get that set up, and then to find a window of time when it made sense for him to meet up with us. We had to time it just right.

He ended up officially moving to Miami the day before his birthday: July 10, 2013. We didn't realize the significance of this until a fan pointed it out on Twitter (you guys really do remember everything, which is amazing): It was *exactly* the three-year anniversary of when we opened our Shoot Us Down channel on YouTube. Very cool. And so hard to believe just how much had happened in that time.

I spent a lot of time on the road that summer and started realizing there are a lot of Mahomies out there! I've always been the kind of person who's really into details—like I notice and pay attention to every little thing. So when I'm in an airport or wherever I am when I'm traveling, I sometimes catch a fan noticing me when they think I can't see them. I watch and I wait for it. Some make a beeline for me, and others look like they're way too nervous or shy and never even say hi. Some even start to cry. I'm always happy to talk to a fan who approaches me, or even take a picture together. I'm so grateful for my fans, and making them happy makes me happy, too.

I also got to go overseas for the first time that summer. My first trip was London in July 2013. I was looking forward to traveling outside the United States for the first time, but I wasn't sure if anyone would come to see me, and what the reaction would be if they did.

I ALWAYS MAKE SURE I GET A CHANCE TO TRY OUT SOME NEW THINGS WHILE I'M SOMEPLACE I'VE NEVER BEEN BEFORE. IT'S SO COOL TO SEE DIFFERENT PARTS OF THE WORLD.

My show was the same day I flew in, and I kept trying to prepare myself for the fact that it might not be good, but at least I was getting to travel. *I don't know*, I thought, *this might not be a good turnout. It's a different country. I might have a few fans here, but who knows?*

As we approached the venue, it was total chaos in the street. There were so many people running around. *What is going on?* I thought. *Is there a parade that's happening today?* And then I got out of our vehicle, and there was this huge roar of a crowd, and I realized the chaos in the street was the people waiting to see me. I couldn't believe it—so many people in a different country who wanted to see me. I was so happy.

Since then, I've traveled to Japan, Germany, Sweden, Mexico, Spain, Italy, Brazil, and other great places, and I can tell you this: Fans all around the world are pretty much the same in many ways—they're very energetic and supportive and loving. But there are definitely differences in different places, which I found pretty interesting. In Japan, everyone and everything is very orderly. They don't get in anyone's way. If they're asked to stand behind a line, they'll politely stand there all day. But in Mexico, the energy is different. Much louder. The rules are different in Mexico and the fans go extra hard. Of course, I love all the different types of fans and still can't believe the attention I sometimes get. When I watch it happen, I feel this intense mix of shock and joy that I hope I never get over, because it's the best.

Traveling overseas is really expensive, so we try to make the most of my time. It's like every fifteen-minute window of time is booked while I'm there. That said, I always make sure I get a chance to try out some new things while I'm someplace I've never been before. It's so cool to see different parts of the world. I get to see how other people live. I get to try new foods and take in the culture. I like to come back with different types of stuff from those places. Of course, I loved Milan because of the fashion, and I did a lot of shopping there. Madrid and Germany were both cool. But I think my favorite place to go so far has been Japan. Not only is everyone extremely nice there, but also the food and atmosphere are so different. I wanted to come back with a sword and some ninja stars, but I didn't because, well, you try getting onto a plane with a sword. But I was happy anyhow because I got my favorite thing in Japan: SHOES. They're weird and big and just different, and it was really cool to come back with something people in America have never seen before. Not many people get to travel out of the country and go to as many different places as I do. I'm hoping I'll get to go to more places and continue to explore the world. I really want to go to Australia and Dubai. And probably places I don't even know about yet. I really want to go everywhere.

That fall I was doing my first headlining tour with MTV and it was presented by their Artist to Watch brand. This was a big deal and I was really excited. The first show of the tour was in Miami so we could come off the road and go right into rehearsals at home. For our final run-throughs, we were in the venue where I'd be performing, getting used to the actual stage

I WILL STAY UNTIL MIDNIGHT IF THAT'S HOW LONG IT TAKES TO GET IT RIGHT.

setup and perfecting every little detail. It was all going great.

And then, a few days before the show, all of a sudden I started feeling bad. Like really bad. My throat hurt and I was running a temperature. Because I'd been on the road so much that year, I'd gotten a little run-down a few months earlier and had gone to an ear, nose, and throat specialist, just to be sure everything was good, and had been told everything was okay. So I figured I was just worn-out again and didn't say anything to anyone. But then I started to feel worse.

I was doing my best to power through and keep rehearsing, but I couldn't deny how awful I felt. When I told my mom, she looked in the back of my throat, and she said it was all inflamed. *Now, that can't be good*, I thought. Luckily, Mike's sister is a doctor at the Children's Hospital in Miami (I told you these guys have hookups everywhere), and she got me in to see another throat specialist right away. He ran all these tests and said I had strep and hemorrhaging on my throat. And then he looked at me and delivered the bad news.

"You shouldn't sing for a week," he said.

Devastated, I looked at my mom. The tour was only ten shows in fourteen days—that would wipe out half the shows. But not listening to the doctor meant I could do permanent damage to my vocal cords. We didn't know what to do. I didn't want to disappoint my fans or my team, especially because I had this whole big group of people who'd literally been helping me put together my show for weeks now.

That whole day was really tense. We talked it over with my team. We got on the phone with the label. I was feeling so lousy that day that I had to leave rehearsal, which I never do. I will stay until midnight if that's how long it takes to get it right. And then, the next day, I was so sick that I was in bed all day, running a fever, sweating all over the place, and sleeping. I

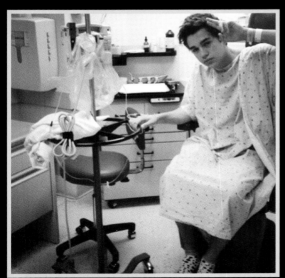
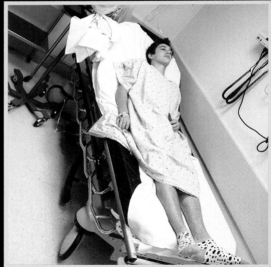

was on medication, but it hadn't kicked in yet, and I couldn't have performed no matter how hard I'd tried. And the show was the next day.

Finally, we all agreed that it was impossible and we needed to reschedule the tour versus me really hurting myself. I *hated* canceling those shows. I'd worked so hard and been so excited for those dates. I was really depressed about it. I felt like I'd let everyone down: my fans, my team, MTV, the production team who'd helped me get the show ready, the other acts on the tour.

After the excitement of traveling so much that year and getting ready for my first big tour, it was hard to suddenly find myself on bed rest. I was literally in bed for three weeks. The doctor had told me not to sing, not to go outside, not to MOVE, basically. At least there was one thing I could do to still make use of my time, because I want to grow as an artist and performer every day of my life. I would go on YouTube and obsessively watch videos of the best performers: Michael Jackson, Usher, Chris Brown, Justin Timberlake, all those guys. And I would study everything: their moves, their facial expressions, the way they carry themselves onstage, *everything*.

There's always so much to learn. Take Michael—he has so much power, and not just in the way he moves, either. I've always felt like his facial expressions are everything. I was watching a Michael video, and I put a piece of paper over his body so just his head was visible, and he was still killing it. Even just with his face, he was able to connect with the audience a hundred percent. Amazing. I was taking mental notes that whole time, and I still work on that.

That's the cool thing about performing, too. It's like a cycle. We all study

This was my first time at a big awards show with stars I'd listened to growing up. Only now I was sitting in the audience with them.

the greats who have come before us, and we take stuff from them, and we make it our own. And then it becomes a part of our show, and eventually, in a way, it becomes ours. I really think that's the best way to grow as an artist and entertainer.

I made good use of my time while I was getting better, but as soon as I got clearance from my doctor, I was beyond ready to get back out there. Luckily, that September, I got to get out there again in one of the biggest, coolest ways possible. I'd been nominated for a VMA, and I got to not only go to the ceremony and walk the red carpet, but also perform. I'd already been at the first annual Radio Disney Music Awards that year, which was so cool and had officially been my first awards show. But the VMAs are different, and I knew EVERYONE was going to be there.

My performance was at the preshow, which took place on the street outside the arena in Brooklyn, New York. I definitely think it's important

to do something cool that people will never forget whenever possible, but there is only so much you can do outside, with no set. I almost never get nervous, but I was definitely feeling a little jittery that day. This was a big deal. This was my first time at a big awards show I'd only ever seen on TV attended by stars I'd listened to growing up. Only now I was sitting in the audience with them.

A lot of artists I admire were there that day. I was glad to get my performance out of the way early so I could just enjoy myself.

During a commercial break, people got up out of their seats and were

just walking around the theater saying hey to people. It was amazing. And then I looked up and there she was, my celebrity crush, Rihanna. Before I could think better of it, I was up out of my seat and over in front of where she was sitting. She looked up at me.

"Hey, Rihanna, my name's Austin," I said. "Nice to meet you."

"Hello," she said, looking at me like, *Who is this kid? Get out of here.*

"I'm a big fan," I said.

"Thanks," she said.

Then I just stood there awkwardly, smiling at her. I think I scared her

a little bit, because I just popped up from nowhere, and she had no idea what was happening or who I was. Finally, I was like, *Okay, I'm going to go sit back down.* Then I left. *All right, that didn't go so well,* I thought as I went back to my seat.

It was fun, though. That was a good time, probably the best night of my life. I know I'm always saying that, but believe me, it's hard to pick just one best night when so many amazing things are happening.

Soon, it was time for my category: Artist to Watch. Everything had

It was a huge day, in a year filled with huge days.

already been so amazing that it almost didn't matter if I won, but of course I wanted to. And then, I couldn't believe it, they were actually calling my name and I was making my way to the podium, and it was all happening.

Yeah, that literally might have been the best night of my life so far.

Just after the VMAs I hired a new vocal coach, Raab, who works with Justin Timberlake and my girl Rihanna, and immediately I could tell he was helping me grow. I dropped my new single "Banga! Banga!" on November 10, and that's always the best feeling—putting new music out into the world. It had more of an urban vibe than what I'd put out before, but it felt like a fun next step for me. For a while, I was trying

to find The Sound that fits my voice perfectly, a sound that's mine, but I like trying out so many different types of music because I truly love so many different types of music, so here's what I've realized: Maybe my sound isn't supposed to be just one thing.

Even though I didn't think it was possible, life was about to get even better. On Thanksgiving that year, not only was I living out my childhood dream of being in New York City for the Macy's Thanksgiving Day Parade, but I was actually performing "Banga! Banga!" on a float in the parade. I was *in the parade*.

That whole day was amazing—well, except for one thing: It was *cold*, like freezing. I was bundled up like crazy, and I was still having a hard time keeping warm. Not that the cold or anything else could have brought me down that day. It was just incredible, the excitement as all the final touches were being put on the floats just before we took off, and then that unbelievable feeling of being in the city, with all that energy, and the streets packed with thousands and thousands of people for blocks and blocks. Not only that, but I soon realized that a lot of them were there to see me. At one point while I was waving to people, out of the corner of my eye I saw this one girl on the other side of the barricade that was keeping the crowd back from the parade route. The next thing I knew, she hurdled the barricade, just hopped over it, and did a full-on sprint toward the float. She was running with everything

she had. And then, still out of the corner of my eye, I saw a cop also full-on sprinting toward her. As soon as he reached her, he wrapped his arms around her and BOOM, he tackled her. She hit the float and then she was down on the ground. *Oh my God, she's on the ground*, I thought. I felt so bad. I could tell it had knocked the breath out of her. But you know what? She hopped back up and stuck out her hand, and I high-fived her. Even after everything, she walked away smiling.

The best thing about that day, though, was that my mom and granddad and aunt Lisa all came out to the parade, and it brought back so many memories. The only person missing was Mema. That was really hard for all of us. But I knew she would have been proud of me, and that meant a lot to me. It was a huge day, in a year filled with huge days.

Once again, it was crazy to see how much everything could change in only one year. I wrapped up 2013 by doing another Jingle Ball run, which meant another chance to travel and perform for new crowds and meet as many fans as possible. I moved from the small stage to the big stage and performed later in the show. And I could tell there were more Mahomies there (btw, I notice all your posters and T-shirts, even from these big stages, and it means the world to me). It was still hard to believe I was sharing a stage with people like Pitbull, Selena Gomez, and Paramore, but it was something I definitely could get used to.

When I got asked to sing "Silent Night" on *Late Night with Jimmy Fallon* just before Christmas, I saw it as an honor and an opportunity. I loved that show, so being a guest on it was awesome. It was also the first time since way back in the beginning that I just sang without all the choreography. I'm always dancing or running around. But this time, it wasn't about the spectacle. It was all about

my voice. And that song is no joke, either. It felt like I was being recognized as a real singer. And that's really important to me. Music is my life, and in order to build a meaningful career, making the best-quality music I can is my priority.

In the meantime, I've continued to have some more amazing firsts. One of the most meaningful ones was writing a song with Robert. We wrote "All I Ever Need" together, and it was such a cool experience. He's become an important part of my musical process in the past year. Not only is it amazing to collaborate with someone who I know so well and who has my back—and I mean going back to the Pop Warner football days, you know?—but

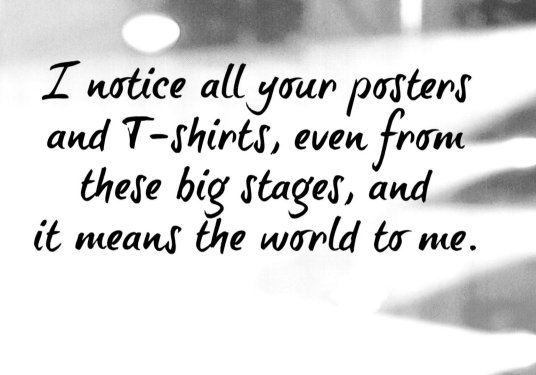

I notice all your posters and T-shirts, even from these big stages, and it means the world to me.

also I'm aware that to show what I can do as an artist, it's going to be crucial for me to record material I can really make my own. And what could be more a reflection of me than a song I wrote with one of my best friends?

I was able to reschedule the MTV Artist to Watch Tour I had to cancel in the fall of 2013 because of my major run-in with strep, which meant I was finally headlining my first tour. We didn't get a chance to do the whole country, but all those dates were amazing.

I had started gearing up for my EP in January 2014, when I put out "Mmm Yeah," featuring Pitbull. We made two videos for that song—a fun lyric video and the official one. That song became my biggest single so far. Then, on my birthday, I announced my summer tour and the date my EP would

BEING THE HEADLINER CARRIES WITH IT A LOT OF RESPONSIBILITY, AND I WAS FULLY PREPARED FOR IT.

be released: May 27. When the time came, I got to perform on *The Today Show* on Memorial Day, as part of their outdoor summer concert series. I'd already been on *The Today Show* once, when "What About Love" came out, and it was an honor to be invited back, especially because I grew up watching it. It was cool to be back in New York City, performing outside Rockefeller Center again. And it was a great way to debut a couple songs off my EP *The Secret*.

We spent months getting everything in place for the Secret tour. which would be my first national headlining tour. This was a big deal, a chance to reach more fans than ever before. We put attention into even the smallest details. I wanted everything to be just right for you, my biggest fans.

One of the big decisions we faced was who the opening acts were going to be. There were a lot of factors to consider. They had to be great

performers, but different from each other so there was something for everyone. They also had to be cool and their teams had to be cool, since we would be spending a lot of time together over the next couple months. The final package was The Vamps, Fifth Harmony, and Shawn Mendes for the first nineteen shows and then Fifth Harmony, Shawn Mendes, and Alex Angelo the last eleven.

Just a year earlier, I'd been the opener for Taylor Swift, and now I was the one getting to pick artists that I respected to come on tour. Not that I was playing crazy-big venues like Taylor, but I still considered it a privilege to be able to invite an artist to join me on the road like she had done for me.

Being the headliner carries with it a lot of responsibility, and I was fully prepared for it.

I t might be a weird thing to say, but I don't really feel like I have a home. There's no place that feels like where I live all the time. Sometimes, I feel like my home is a hotel room. That's pretty much where I am on most days, and I literally live out of a suitcase (actually more like three or four). I live on the road. But, for me, right now, that's okay.

I think a huge part of feeling at home on the road has to do with the fact that I'm traveling with my team. My extended family. So, wherever I am, it feels like I've got a solid home base, even if I'm moving around on a tour bus. I really think being around good people is the secret to a quality life, especially in this industry. I am so fortunate to have this core group of family and friends to be there with me and support me. I know they keep me grounded.

I was thinking about this a lot going into my big summer 2014 tour, because we were launching it somewhere with real significance

12. HOMECOMING

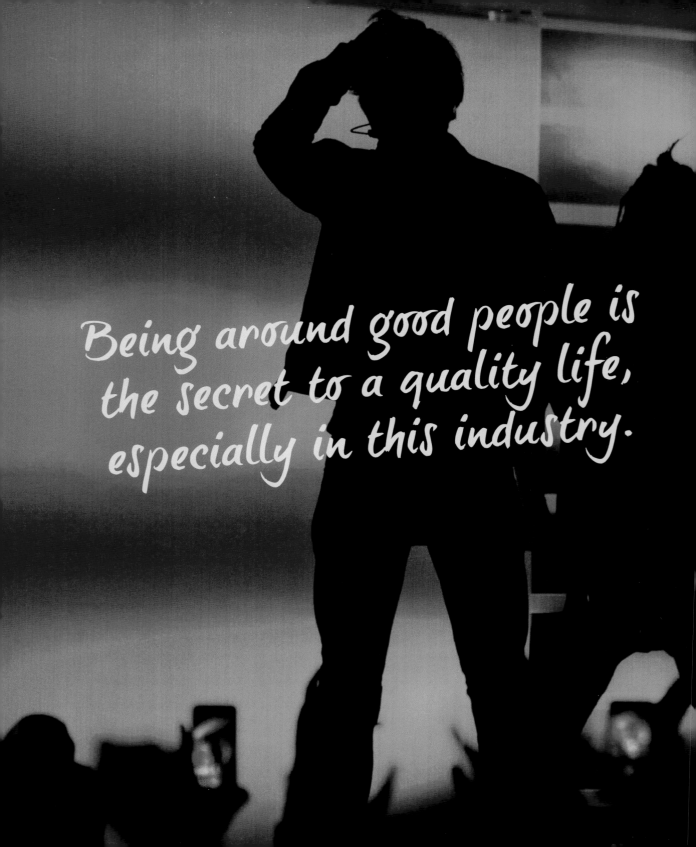

Being around good people is the secret to a quality life, especially in this industry.

for me: San Antonio. And it felt amazing to be kicking off my tour with a sold-out show in my hometown, at the same place where I'd gone to the rodeo with my family as a kid.

We flew into San Antonio on Sunday and spent all week rehearsing with my choreographer, Nick, and his assistant, Aubree. And of course Josh was with us. I always feel better when I know he's backing me up.

My vocal coach, Raab, came to work with me one-on-one. A lot of times he and I use FaceTime to warm up right before a show. But for the really special events, he flies in. And for this one he was going extra hard to warm me up. For good reason, too.

It's definitely a challenge, singing and dancing at the same time. You're already losing a lot of breath from dancing, and then you have to sing. And sound good. If I've been off the road for a little while, when I first get back into rehearsing and performing, I'm just dead every night after the show. So one of the first priorities that week was conditioning. Luckily, we had a huge empty arena to work with.

Raab would sit in one of the empty seats with his mini-keyboard and play scales in order for me to do my vocal exercise to warm up. And then he got down to it.

"On your mark, get set, go," he said.

With that I sprinted around the perimeter of the arena's balcony, as fast as I possibly could, to build up my lung capacity. The entire time, he was talking into a microphone that fed into an earbud in my ear, giving me a sort of pep talk.

And then, right when I came around the final curve and reached him again, I had to stop in front of him and sing. See, it isn't enough to have the best breath capacity possible. I also have to deliver vocally, even when I'm already exhausted, and sound as good as I do when I'm singing in the studio. That's the goal. So we did this again and again. It's like music boot camp.

Meanwhile, the entire arena was alive with activity. The set was being built. Equipment was being tested. And Nick worked out the dancers on the stage, running through their moves with them, so they'd have them down when it was time for us to rehearse together. You wouldn't believe how many times we run through even the tiniest details—and in an hour-long show, that's a lot of details—because they all add up to an amazing experience, but having just one little thing go wrong can throw the whole thing off. You might not notice. But we do, and we want it to be perfect for you.

Luckily, there are these little pockets of downtime during the day, which helps me to stay in shape mentally going into a big show. Sometimes these moments are filled up, too. There are always interviews to be done, and tons of decisions to be made about what I'm going to wear, what order I'm going to sing the songs in, and even what microphone I'm going to use. So when there's a chance to chill for a few minutes, I take it. That's why it's so great, in the middle of all this craziness, to have AC, Robert, and Zach on the road with me.

It's really important to keep everything moving on these long rehearsal days, and even so, we're often still going through the set at eleven o'clock at night, even if I had an eight thirty call time in the lobby of my hotel that morning, in order to do all the promotional TV and radio appearances that

also go into putting on a big show. So when I'm given a break, I take it. Usually AC, Robert, and Zach are right there with me.

It's pretty amazing because, even though everything has changed, really nothing has. They're still my same crew, and I'm so glad to be able to depend on them for that. Like, for example, if I ever need fashion advice, I'll go to AC. His dream is to be an actor, but he's been getting into fashion lately.

Now, if I need advice about a girl, I'll go to Robert. He always has good advice. And, of course, more and more these days, Robert is also the one I go to for questions about my music. Since "All I Ever Need," he and I have been writing together a lot. Plus, he does the rap in "Shawty Shawty," so he's on the road performing with me, too.

Zach, I can count on for anything. But what he's best at is making us all laugh. I don't even know what I'd do if they weren't with me on this journey.

Over the next few days, I literally rehearse every single element of the show, from how to hold the mic stand (seriously—Nick and I worked on this for forty-five minutes one day) to the wardrobe change that comes halfway into the set. I've got just over a minute when I don't have to be onstage and my wardrobe person isn't convinced I can make the switch. So she has me practice in my dressing room while timing me. When I prove I've got it down, I get the okay to change outfits, just like I wanted to. Like I said, I'm into details. We all are.

Even though there's so much to nail down and not nearly enough time to do it, I still sneak away for my most important ritual. During the second day of rehearsal, I find a minute when I can be alone, which isn't always easy on the road, and I make the long walk to the seats farthest away from the stage. When I sit down and look out at the stage where I'll be performing, it's almost like I can see all the rodeos I've been to there, and everything that happened between those childhood outings and this dream life I'm living. It feels amazing.

The days are long, but the time goes by fast. Before I know it, it's the day of the show. Everyone's on edge because we're not going to get to run through the show again like we hoped, which basically means our show tonight will be like a dress rehearsal.

When everyone starts arriving, it's this amazing feeling, like there's a

WHEN I SIT DOWN
AND LOOK OUT AT THE
STAGE WHERE I'LL
BE PERFORMING, IT'S
ALMOST LIKE I CAN
SEE ALL THE RODEOS
I'VE BEEN TO THERE,
AND EVERYTHING THAT
HAPPENED BETWEEN
THOSE CHILDHOOD
OUTINGS AND THIS
DREAM LIFE I'M LIVING.

Even when I'm backstage, I swear I can tell the minute the audience starts walking into the building. It's like the doors open and there's this immediate charge in the air.

buzz in the air. The opening acts roll up just before sound check, and suddenly catering is full of the British accents of The Vamps, the laughter of the girls in Fifth Harmony, and Shawn Mendes eating with his team. Everyone's talking about the tour and making tonight special. Not to mention the fact that Granddad and Aunt Lisa are there, and the parents of all my boys. It's definitely like a family reunion tonight.

During sound check, I sit in one of the front rows and watch at least a few songs by each of the performers. Like I said, I can very clearly remember how, not that long ago, I was in their shoes, and so I always want to show my respect

by catching their set, which I don't always have time to do once the show gets under way later in the night. Plus, there's always the chance to learn.

That afternoon, my VIP meet and greet goes well. These always include an intimate preshow performance for several hundred fans, plus Robert runs the Q&A part of it. I love doing these because I get to play different versions of songs from my regular set for the fans—like an acoustic version of "Mmm Yeah," for example. And then I get to meet everyone and take pictures.

I'm getting ready for the meet-and-greet part when Dave comes to my dressing room to tell me that one of my fans started feeling sick and almost fainted. The medical crew had stabilized her and she was okay, but they were going to have her parents come pick her up. That was the problem. She had missed the VIP sound check party while she was being treated, and now she was going to miss the meet and greet and the concert.

Dave and I walked to where she was by the front of the stage. She was in a wheelchair while she waited to get picked up. When she saw me, her face immediately crumpled. She put her hand over her eyes to cover her tears.

"Oh my God, oh my God, oh my God," she said.

I walked up to her and smiled at her as gently as I could.

"Hey there," I said. "How are you feeling?"

I reached down and moved the wheelchair's footrests, and helped her stand so we could get a photo. With me holding her up a little bit, and her friend on the other side of her, she finally relaxed enough to smile. Those are the moments that make all the hard work worth it.

Meet and greets are always fun, but this was one of the best ones I've ever done. My San Antonio fans were extra thoughtful—one girl brought me a numbered table tag from my favorite restaurant, Whataburger, printed with my lucky number 74, and another girl brought me a pizza. Plus, there were so many familiar faces: old friends and neighbors and even my old guitar teacher, Manny. It felt amazing to show him how much his instruction had helped me and where it had finally led me.

Even when I'm backstage, I swear I can tell the minute the audience starts walking into the building. It's like the doors open and there's this immediate charge in the air. I can feel all your excitement and emotion, and I get filled up with excitement and emotion, too. That's the power of music. It's such a great way to connect with people, and it means so much to me that you get it, too, and love my music as much as you do.

I wouldn't say I was nervous exactly as the clock ticked down, but I was definitely nerved up. So I distracted myself by playing basketball with AC and a few dancers who weren't busy doing their own preshow routines. As we played, the first opening band suddenly drowned out the sound of the basketball against the cement floor. It's showtime.

I walked away from the prayer circle with everyone's claps and shouts still ringing in my ears. I've always really loved that moment. We're all in it together, all riding that particular mix of adrenaline and extreme focus that goes into putting on a really good show. I walked into my dressing room and put my in-ears in, which allow me to hear communications from my crew while I'm onstage. I bounced up and down in my shoes a few times, making sure I was ready to go out there and show my hometown exactly how far I'd come and just how far I could take what had once seemed like a crazy dream to most people.

As I walked up to the backstage area, everyone in my camp patted me on the back or gave me a little nod or word of encouragement. But no one tried to really talk to me. They knew this was my time, one of the most important moments in my day, when I go into my zone and take everything I'd practiced and perfected and use it to get ready to let it soar out of me in order to connect with all of you.

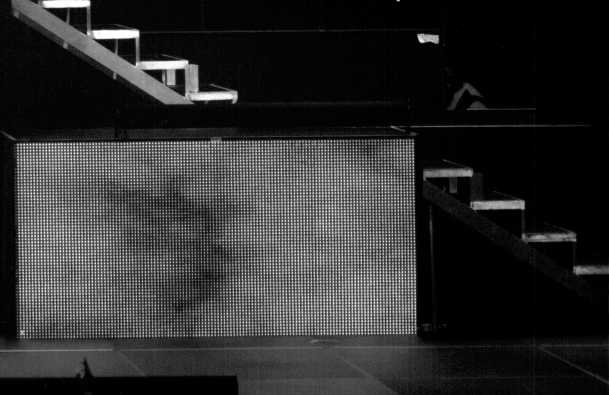

I was ready to go out there and show my hometown exactly how far I'd come and just how far I could take what had once seemed like a crazy dream to most people.

I STOPPED AND LISTENED TO THE CROWD SCREAMING AND THOUGHT ABOUT HOW FAR I'D COME AND EVERYONE WHO HAD HELPED ME ALONG THE WAY TO GET HERE, HOW MUCH I'D NEEDED TO BELIEVE IN MYSELF, AND HOW MUCH THEY'D SUPPORTED ME WITH THEIR BELIEF.

It was dark backstage, but I knew exactly where everything and everyone was—exactly where it was all supposed to be—and I felt myself fit into the space at the heart of the show that was just for me, right where I belonged, leading my team, singing for my Mahomies, living my dream.

Just a few feet away but invisible in the blackness, girls shrieked and screamed, and I could feel that wave of energy that had first rushed into the building hours ago. It was incredible, this preshow rush, not just on any night in any town, but on the first night of my first national headlining tour, and in my hometown of San Antonio.

I positioned myself behind the screen doors that would open in a few minutes, through which I would walk out and perform for my fans. I stopped and listened to the crowd screaming and thought about how far I'd come and everyone who had helped me along the way to get here, how much I'd needed to believe in myself, and how much they'd supported me with their belief. Dazed, tears pressing against the backs of my eyes, I let it all fill me up. And then I shook it off.

It all came down to the one thing I'd always loved more than anything else: the music.

Through the arena's PA, a voice boomed:

"AUSTIN MAHONE!"

The beat started up, the door opened, and I stepped out onto my stage, ready to put on a show people would never forget.

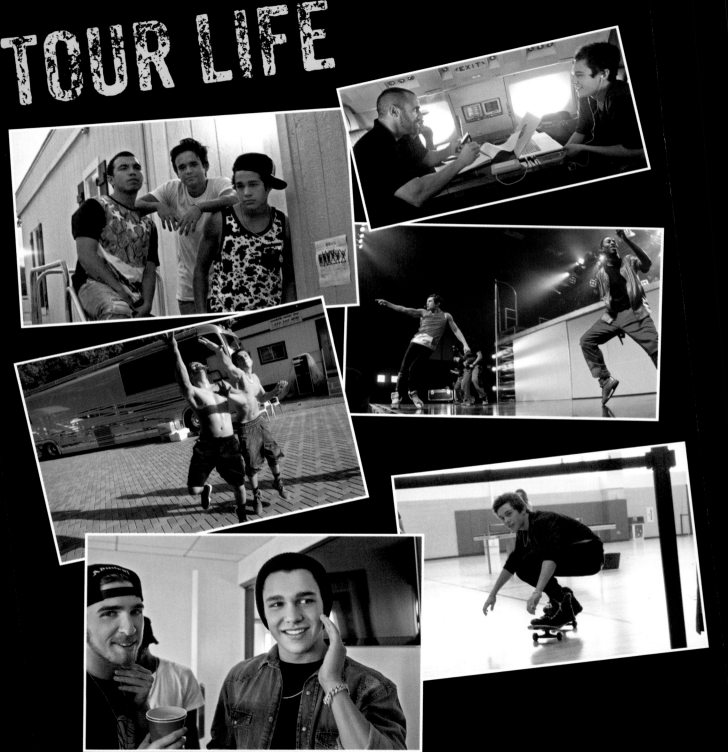

TOUR LIFE

COVER OUTTAKES

My world has grown so much in the last few years. It used to be me and my mom doing everything—now we're surrounded by an amazing group of people who help out in so many different ways. I couldn't do what I do without them, which includes making this book.

I definitely couldn't have done it without my mom or my crew—C, Robert, and Zach—who spent hours going through old pictures and scanned them, e-mailed them, and did whatever it took to get them into the book.

My management team—Rocco, Dave, Mike, and Brian—helped me figure out this whole book thing, and they were with me every step of the way. Also want to thank my head of security, Joe, for helping to make it happen and Dan Roof and Erica Gerard for getting the word out.

I want to thank Sarah Tomlinson, Farrin Jacobs, Sasha Illingworth, Wendy Dopkin, Jonathan Lopes, and everyone at Little, Brown for working so hard to put it all together.

Thanks also to my label, Chase Records/Cash Money/Republic, for your continued support, and to the team at Paradigm.

I'm grateful that my family supports me in everything I do. Thank you, Granddad, Aunt Lisa, Nana, Aunt Robin, Rylie, and Logan.

And, of course, none of this would be possible without my fans. You are truly the best, and I can't thank you enough for supporting me. I hope I'm making you proud.

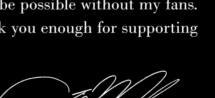

PHOTO CREDITS